Rock House

Presents

LEAD
SINGER
From Start to Stage

Written & Method By
John McCarthy

T0105929

Adapted By: Jimmy Rutkowski
Supervising Editor: John McCarthy
Music Transcribing & Engraving: Jimmy Rutkowski
Production Manager: John McCarthy
Layout, Graphics & Design: Jimmy Rutkowski
Photography: Rhonda Rutkowski
Models: Damiano Scarfi, Mary Kuchar
Music Consultant: Sarah Golley
Copy Editor: Cathy McCarthy

Cover Art Direction & Design:
Jimmy Rutkowski

HL281651
Produced by McCarthy Publishing®

Table of Contents

Icon Key

There will be icons placed at the beginning of many lessons in this book. These icons tell you there are additional information, audio backing tracks and demonstrations and/or learning utilities available to help you learn and practice that lesson most effectively. You can access and download this support content at our Lesson Support website when you register your book using the member number **LS829243** at: **RockHouseMethod.com**.

Backing Track

Backing track icons are placed on lessons where there is an audio demonstration to let you hear what that lesson should sound like or a backing track tor you to sing the vocal exercise along with. Use these audio tracks to guide you through the lessons. Practice with them repetitively every day.

Video

Video icons are placed on lessons where there is a video available to let you see and hear what that lesson should sound like and for you to sing the vocal exercise along with. Use these videos to guide you through the lessons. Practice with them repetitively every day.

Digital eBook

When you register this product at the Lesson Support site RockHouseMethod. com, you will receive a digital version of this book. This interactive eBook can be used on all devices that support Adobe PDF. This will allow you to access your book using the latest portable technology any time you want.

Use this member number at RockHouseMethod.com to register for FREE Lesson Support, Backing Tracks, & Video Content.

Member Number LS829243

Introduction

Congratulations for taking the first step to improve your singing. In this course book I will cover a wide spectrum of techniques that will help you sing with a strong voice and increase your range to hit higher and lower notes easier. You will also learn how to sing with a rich full tone by using your voice the proper way.

Before we get started with the course I want you to assess your voice to see where you are now before you jump in. I will also ask you to assess your progress a few times during the course that will be noted. It is important as you are progressing in your career that you assess your progress to see what is working and what is not. You need to continuously fine-tune your skills to progress to your full capacity.

John McCarthy

Chapter 1
Analyze Your Voice

Increase your Range. Using any musical instrument measure your vocal range to find the highest and lowest note you can sing comfortably when starting this course. As you go through the course you will be learning exercises that will increase your range. The goal is to train your voice so you can sing at the highest level and expand your range higher and lower singing notes with ease.

If you have access to a piano or guitar these two instruments will provide an easy way to measure your range as you start this course. As you progress though the course you should continue to measure your range and you will clearly see the progress you make after working with your exercises for a period of time. An average person has about an octave to an octave and a half vocal range. Our goal will be to help you sing two octaves and higher.

Build Tone & Resonance. Record your voice to hear the tonal qualities. The way you sing will alter the tone your voice creates. Tone is how full your voice sounds. Does your voice have a deep full bass tone or does it have a high pitched thin sound? You will learn exercises that will help you sing and support your notes to sing with a strong full tone.

Sing a Song. Pick a song to sing and record yourself. This will be another way to see your progress as you go through this course. Choose a song you can sing comfortably and record it, you will sing the same song later in the course so you can compare your voice and see the progress.

Chapter 2
Stretches

Your voice is a very sensitive, irreplaceable instrument. Proper care is needed so that fatigue, strain and, injury can be avoided. Before you begin any practice sessions, I recommend that you warm up your body in order to be as comfortable as possible and sing effectively. Warming up your voice is very important. Just like a runner stretches and relaxes their body before running a race to run at their highest potential you need to stretch and relax your body before you sing so you can sing at your highest level. Warming up will help you to reduce strain, which can harm your voice. If your body is tense and tight when you sing you can cause damage to your vocal folds. Warm ups will also help to reduce and even eliminate vocal fatigue. This fatigue is when your voice feels tired from singing for a period of time and occurs frequently when you're not warmed up properly and relaxed. Being relaxed properly will also help improve the fullness of your upper register voice making belting easier. To prepare lets get your blood flowing with stretches.

Tension can be detrimental to your capacity to sing. Keep in mind just how many large and small muscles you are flexing, and the amount of energy it requires to engage all of those muscles while belting out your favorite tunes!

When you sing you are creating muscle resistance, which in turn causes tension. It is therefore important to warm up those muscles and prepare them to help you sing at the highest level. The most effective way to prepare to sing is by stretching and using vocal warm up exercises to reduce stress, relax your muscles and fine-tune your body. When you sing if your muscles are too tight you will sound out of tune and tense. This can also cause harm to your voice. You need to take care of your voice to get optimum performance.

To start I am going to show you some simple and fun stretches you can use to get warmed up and ready to sing the night away! Some may look and feel a little silly, but I assure you they are highly effective.

Full Body Stretches

Lets start with some full body stretches to get your body ready to sing at peak performance!

Chest Stretch

To do this stretch you can sit or stand. Lace your fingers together behind your lower back. Take a deep breath in, hold for 15-20 seconds and slowly exhale, while pressing your elbows behind you as far as you can, squeezing your shoulder blades together. Arch your back slightly to stretch out your chest, abs, and shoulders. Be sure to exhale fully, relax and repeat.

Chest Stretch Variation 2

Do the same stretch while lacing you fingers behind your neck, Take a deep breath in, and slowly exhale while pressing your elbows back as far as you can. Squeeze your shoulder blades together and feel your chest stretch.

Neck Stretch

Having your neck properly stretched will help relax your throat as well as your neck. Start by tilting your head to the left. Bring your left hand up and over your head and place it on the top right side of your head. Take a deep breath in and as you exhale, gently press downward. You can also increase the stretch process on your left side of your neck by dropping your right shoulder. Hold the stretch position for 20 seconds and then repeat this on the right side next. Make sure to push gently and don't force your head downward; if you feel any pain stop immediately.

Hip Stretch

Stretching your hips will help to open up your lower body and keep your midsection loose. Get a comfortable chair and sit near the edge. Place your left ankle across your right knee. Then place your right hand on the top of the left knee. Take a deep breath in. As you exhale, gently press the knee downward to stretch the outer left hip. Hold this stretch for 20 seconds or until you feel comfortable with the stretch. Once you finish repeat the same process with your other side.

Lower Back Stretch

Stretching your back is important to help to relax your upper body. Lie down on your back. Keep your left leg straight on the floor. Bend your right knee inward toward your head and hold it. Gently clasp your hands on top of your right shin right below your knee. Slowly pull your knee towards your chest and hold the stretch for 15-20 seconds. Repeat the same process on the other side. This will release tension in your lower back, hips, and backside.

Small Muscle Stretches

Once we have comfortably loosened up the larger muscles, we can begin to prepare the tinier muscles that will directly support our voice. Let's get started with these now.

The Yawn

You've been yawning your entire life, but it's probably been when you were tired in the past. I know it may not be easy but now I need you to yawn on command. As you are yawning I want you to pay attention to the inside of your throat and the stretching feeling starting from the base of your jaw. This opens up your airway and your throat. This is not necessarily the way you want to sing, but it is a warm up exercise to relax your throat, diaphragm and release tension. Do this for a few minutes until you start to feel relaxed. Yawning will also help to raise the soft pallet (the soft fleshy part at the top of your throat). This creates a vocal release in the throat, lowering the tension and possibility of constriction. Take full and deep yawns for this to be most effective. Repeat this for a few minutes, but don't fall asleep!

Say Cheese!

A great way to stretch the muscles in your face is to just smile repetitively. There are many muscles you use to smile believe it or not! Start by holding your lips shut, and then try slowly raising the corners of your mouth as much as you possibly can. Repeat this several times. On a side note, an added bonus of this exercise is you will realize that you actually start to feel happier when you smile.

Pucker Those Lips Up!

Now its time to stretch those lips! Your lips play a significant role in your singing ability and having them ready to rock will help you sing better. Your lips are the final exit point for any words, letters, or sounds that you want to produce. The proper placement of the lips and their proper form is essential to producing a final, pure and fluid sound. Controlling the lips may seem like an easy task because you do it all the time. But when it comes to singing, the lips have to be managed much more carefully. You will shape your lips distinctly to pronounce each and every syllable. Start by pretending to park a wet one on your significant other, so to speak. Then try sucking your lips in as much as possible into your mouth. Believe it or not, there are 3 muscles groups that control lip movement, and this is how you stretch them. You can have a lot of fun with this stretch!

Jaw Stretch

This stretch will supplement the yawn stretch, warming up and relaxing the same muscles. Move the bottom of your jaw up, down and side-to-side. Concentrate on staying relaxed as you do this, keeping your jaw as loose as possible. You should massage the jaw on both sides up at the hinge point under your ears first to loosen the jaw muscles. Try to wiggle the jaw loosely as well to make sure it is ready for the stretches.

Raise an Eyebrow

In addition to your eyes this stretch will work many other muscles in your scalp, nose and jaw. Part of relaxing your face is to warm up the muscles in your eyes. Start the stretch by raising and lowering your eyebrows 10 to 15 times. You should start to notice the other muscles in your scalp, nose and jaw moving as well. Repeat this for a few minutes daily.

The Eye Roll

Here is another eye stretch exercise. Move your eyes up and down repetitively. Take your time and try not to move your head. Next move you eyes side to side. Finally roll your eyes round and round.

Chapter 3
Posture

Posture is the Foundation for all Good Singing

My goal is to teach you how to sing with a freely produced, rich, open and resonated sound, and it all begins with learning posture that will help you progress comfortably. Proper posture allows your body and voice to be relaxed and tension free. I'm going to give you a few exercises to help you develop great posture and build your base to excel as a singer.

Getting Ready to Rock

First stand in front of a mirror and analyze your posture to make sure you are relaxed as you get ready to sing. Don't hunch up your shoulders, drop or raise your chin, or tighten your jaw. When looking in the mirror your stance should be upright with your shoulders relaxed, hands loosely by your side, eyes looking straight ahead with your chin at a normal angle. Many singers make the mistake of presuming they must make weird rocker faces to sing with attitude but this is not true because it will just tense your face and body, a good singer is one who looks and sounds relaxed and natural.

Exercise and Posture Drill

Start by standing up as straight as possible with your spine stretched tall and try to envision the top of your head trying to touch the ceiling.

Put your arms out and horizontal to floor with your palms facing down. Hold your shoulder blades back but don't make them overly tense.

Put one foot slightly ahead of the other, with your weight balanced forward on the balls of both feet.

Keep your knees unlocked, flexible and loose.

Tilt your pelvis downward and slightly forward.

Next turn your arms so that the palms are facing toward the ceiling.

You should feel an extra stretch that occurs in your ribs. Your chest should now be very wide, separated and raised, with space between the bottom of the ribs and your waistline.

Keeping everything in position lower your arms to a normal position by your side.

The back of your neck back should feel like it is pulled backward against an imaginary wall.

Once you have this posture set you must remember it and make it come natural to you. Walk around the room with some attitude and feel the power! Repeat this posture drill repetitively and make sure it is comfortable and feels natural. **"Repetition is the mother of skill!"**

Common Posture Problems

Locking the Knees

Many singers don't realize the things they do with their bodies when they sing. One common problem is when your knees are locked. This is a problem because it also makes your body off balance. This in turn causes body tension and will make you tense when you sing. Bend your knees slightly and put your weight forward on the balls of the feet. Keep your back straight and don't slouch. You must take notice and avoid unintentional locking of the knees.

Rock Back

Another common problem singers can face is pulling the shoulders back too much and tightening them up. This results in tense shoulders and a unbalanced signing position. You should use the muscles around the rib cage to lift the ribs up from the waistline. The intercostal muscles surrounding the rib cage are the muscles that should be used to lift the ribs and the sternum. So this posture you don't want occurs when the shoulders are pulled back instead of lifting the sternum high, and your backside is not tucked under instead it is pushed backward. In this tense, unbalanced position, it will be difficult to have great vocal production.

Chest Slouch

When you sing, air is exhaled and in the process it is easy to allow the chest to cave in and the rib cage to drop backward. If this occurs as you sing you will lose the height of the sternum and this will result in unsupported singing. As you sing a phrase, consciously retain the height of the sternum and resist the collapse of the rib cage.

There are other posture problems but these three are the most common ones. You should continuously monitor your posture by singing in front of a full-length mirror to analyze your posture. Check all of the important topics we discussed such as placement of the feet, weight shifting, loose knee position and keeping your body natural and relaxed.

Achieving a good singing posture will make a noticeable difference in the overall sound of your voice. You must master the correct singing posture and practice it repetitively and then you will notice a significant improvement in the quality of your voice. Your body will then be prepared to work on the next key ingredient needed on your mission to become a great singer, breathing.

Chapter 4
Breathing Exercises

Air, Fuel for Your Voice

Air is the fuel for singing. The tone we create when we sing rests on a cushion of air and the way we breathe is the fuel for the sounds we produce. The more control you have over the air flow, the more control you will have over your singing tone. I am going to show you exercises to help you control and support airflow and you will learn how important it is to supply the fuel properly. This is achieved by keeping the upper airway open and relaxed as you sing.

Breathing is Movement

Movement of air, movement of muscles and organs and movement of energy. A healthy strong voice requires free movement of air and all the muscles involved in breathing, and this results in free movement of the vocal folds.

When the airflow is consistent and strong you vocal tone will be strong as well. If your airflow is uncontrolled and inconsistent, your voice will break and waiver. Similar to a kite your voice relies on a consistent airflow to keep rocking strong.

Breathing Like a Singer

What makes breathing for singing different from other breathing is the action of the rib cage. In normal breathing, the rib cage expands to bring in oxygen, then collapses or lowers as the breath is let out. In singing, you want to create a feeling of firm support for the lungs so that as you let the air out, the rib cage does not collapse. It is a feeling of passive resistance keeping the rib cage high and wide and not allowing the ribs to drop into the waistline. As a singer you must learn to inhale quicker and exhale slower than in a reflex, life-breathing situation.

Here's a simple exercise to discover the muscles and organs involved with breathing as a singer:

- Sit in a chair with your feet flat on the floor.
- Lean over and rest your forearms across your knees, relaxing your head, neck and body.
- Inhale slowly and deeply through your nose.
- Feel your back and stomach expand; relax into your lap, while you are expanding your lower abdomen.
- Exhale slowly through your mouth and gently pull your tummy away from your thighs, lifting your abdomen in.
- Let the chest stay relatively still.

> *Repeat this for 3 to 5 minutes. Each time you repeat, move a little toward sitting upright, continuing to breathe, expanding your abdomen and ribs.*

Abdominal Muscle and Breath Support Exercises

While keeping the rib cage high and wide, you use the abdominal muscles for support. As you sing, the diaphragm gradually lifts, pushing air up and out of the lungs as the tone is produced. Because the rib cage is kept high and wide, the diaphragm will lift gradually and you have better control of your breath. Think of your rib cage as an accordion, keeping it expanded, rather than squeezed together.

As you do these exercises, remember to keep the chest and rib cage high, wide and relaxed. You don't want to let all your air out too soon or quickly. Try not to save all your air up until the end of the exercise and then let it explode out in a burst. Note that the basic breathing and posture principles you learned earlier in this program will apply to all the following exercises. You want a consistent stream of air with everything that you do.

Exercise 1 – The Hisser

- To get started you need to stand using the proper posture you learned in the previous section. This will set you up holding the chest high and wide.
- Take a deep breath in through your nose and as you do this expand your rib cage and lungs to capacity.
- Stay relaxed and release any tension in the chest and shoulder area. Next exhale using a hissing sound similar to air escaping from a tire or tube. Let your air our slowly and as you do this count slowly from one to ten.
- Most people feel the reaction to collapse the rib cage while doing this. Resist the inclination while you are exhaling.

Exercise 2 – Breath Discipline

- Inhale through the nose as you expand the rib cage and lungs to capacity.
- Instead of "hissing," count aloud to 20. Work your way up to 40 counts over a period of time.
- The key here is to let as little air out as possible as you count. It is not easy to restrict your air as you count.
- If you hold your hand in front of your mouth as you count you can feel how much air you are releasing and this can help you to control it easier.

Exercise 3 – Emptying the Breath Tank

- Take a deep breath in through your nose and expand your rib cage and lungs to capacity.
- As you let your breath out count out loud very slow from 1 to 6. I want you to use as full and open a voice as possible. You should be constantly feeding the vocal tone a great deal of warm air.
- As you speak each number keep the chest high and wide and think of expanding the rib cage again.
- All your breath should be used up when you finish speaking the last number.
- Repeat this several times until you feel natural doing this exercise.

Exercise 4 – Build the Support Muscle

- The following is an exercise to remind you of the proper muscular feeling you should achieve when keeping the rib cage high and wide.
- Start by placing your right hand just under your ribs in the middle of your chest, right where you feel the inverted V of your rib cage.
- Take a deep breath in.
- Make a fist with your left hand and place it against your mouth and blow gently on the fist but don't allow any air to come out.
- Take notice of your rib expansion and the firmness of your sternum area.

Exercise 5 – The Soft Cough Exercise

I want you to do a gentle cough as if you were clearing your throat and as you are doing this feel the muscle contractions around your lower torso. These muscles are used to support your voice so doing this will wake up the muscles and get them ready to help you sing.

Chapter 5
Vocal Registers

A vocal register is a range of tones in the human voice produced by a particular vibration pattern in the vocal folds. Registers occur because the vocal folds are capable of producing several different vibratory patterns. Each of these vibratory patterns appears within a particular range of pitches and produces certain characteristic sounds. I am going to explain the different vocal registers so you can understand the voice a bit more in depth.

Vocal Fry Register

This is the lowest register that can be attained by the human voice. In many modern singing styles the Vocal Fry is also referred to as a growl that can be added into other registers as well. A distorted rattling, crackling, growling or frying sound quality characterizes the vocal fry. The vocal folds become compact and vibrate as air is forced through them. Singers typically use this mode of singing to obtain pitches at a very low frequency that they may not otherwise be able to access in their chest register. Until recently there has been little mention of the vocal fry register in singing. A distinction should be noted here between the vocal fry register and the vocal fry effect, which is a quality that is added as a stylistic element for brief parts of notes or words or as a complete singing style that is covered in this course as well.

Chest Register

The chest register refers to the natural register of the human voice. It is closely related to your normal speaking voice. Most men speak entirely within their chest register, while most women speak in both their chest and middle registers.

The timbre of chest voice is warmer and darker than that of middle and head voice and it is characterized by darker vowel qualities. The Chest voice has more thick vocal mass more of the vocal folds are involved in phonation within this lower register. The vocal folds are thickest and fattest in the chest register.

Middle Register

The register between chest voice and head voice is called the middle register, or medium voice.

The timbre of this register is generally thought to be a mix of both the chest and the head voice qualities giving it a very warm, rich tone that isn't quite as dark as the chest voice but also not quite as bright as the head voice.

Head Voice Register

The head register lies above the middle register. The term 'head voice' is generally used to describe the feeling that happens when the sound resonates primarily in your head while singing. It has a characteristic 'ringing' tone and modified acoustics.

Head voice is sometimes called the "lighter mechanism'" of the voice because mass reduces as the vocal folds lengthen. As a result, most singers experience a sense of lightening in resonance as they enter the head register.

Falsetto

The term falsetto is most often used in the context of singing to refer to a type of vocal phonation that enables the singer to sing notes beyond the vocal range of the normal or modal voice. Falsetto is a musical term for a male voice that's artificially high. Falsetto means "artificial voice" and comes from the Italian word falso for "false." When men suddenly sing way up high above their speaking voices, it can sound almost fake.

The unique sound of falsetto is produced by the air blowing over the very thin edges of the thyroarytenoid muscle (thin muscle that forms the body of the vocal fold and that supports the wall of the ventricle and its appendix) and the pitch is controlled mostly by a regulation of the breath flow.

Vocal Range Chart

Below is a chart you can use to help you find your vocal range.

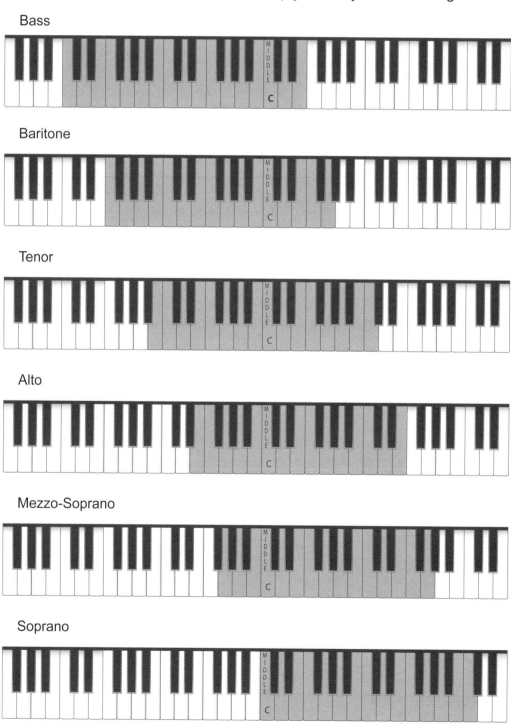

Bass

Baritone

Tenor

Alto

Mezzo-Soprano

Soprano

Chapter 6
Warming Up the Voice

By now you should be all stretched, relaxed and ready to take the next step. Let's slowly warm up your voice in order to get ready for the vocal exercises to follow.

The duration of the warm up time depends on the individual. Some factors include: your physical health, the type of singing you choose and whether you are belting or singing softly. Close your eyes and use your imagination to feel the areas of your body we are targeting in these warm ups. You must be focused on strengthening and increasing the control over each production area.

About the Warm Ups

In the following lessons you will work on a few basic vocal warm up exercises to prepare the muscles in your mouth, throat, tongue and diaphragm.

As you work through these warm-up techniques you will increase your breath control, articulation, projection, range, and tone. Our goal is to make it much easier to produce tones and get you ready to hit the stage!

In this chapter you will learn simple exercises including Lip Rolls, Humming, Slides & Sirens, and Tongue Trills. Practice these exercises repetitively and use them as part of your daily practice routine.

It is very helpful to watch the video demonstration of each exercise to get the exact way to preform the exercise. This will allow you to get the most out of each exercise and you will see the best results quickly. As you perform each of these exercises make sure to use proper posture, stand balanced while keeping your feet flat on the floor a shoulders width apart. You should take deep breaths to use the full power of your diaphragm.

<u>Humming Vocal Exercises</u>

Humming is a great vocal warm up! In fact, it's one of the best all-around vocal exercises. Humming can be done almost anytime, anywhere because it's quieter. When doing closed mouth vocal exercises the tone is emerging from the nasal passages and not the mouth and does not project like open mouth singing. The basic principle is to resonate the voice with gently closed lips while holding your teeth apart. You need to stay relaxed with no tightness of lips, jaw, tongue, facial muscles, neck or shoulders. The only thing that you should feel is the abdominal support muscles coming into play as should happen in any singing. For humming you need to get what I call "The Buzz in your Face" This is where you generate a vibration in the middle of your face and your nasal passage.

Humming will boost the "internal resonance" your vocal chords create. The following exercises will raise your capacity to hear and better understand your tone internally, enabling you to tune your notes before you begin singing. This is very important because it correctly enhances the positioning of the diaphragm, mouth, throat and nasal passages. Begin by making a Mmmm sound. You should allow the pitch to shift upwards as you hum.

As your pitch increases, you will start to feel a buzzing like feeling in your nose. You may even feel it in your eyes, all the way to your head. One thing that makes this exercise great is you feel you voice vibrating inside you and you become more familiar with your own voice this way!

Humming Exercise – Whole Step Intervals

In this next exercise you will hum up whole step Intervals. While doing a hum exercise like this you slide or slur up and down to the notes while keeping the humming Mmmm sound resonating. This exercise will start on middle "C" then move up the scale. Make sure to use the audio backing track to sing along.

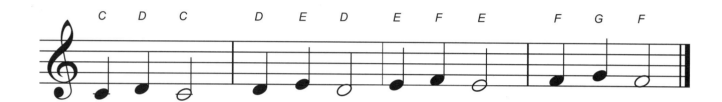

Humming Exercise – Up the Triads

The final humming exercise will go up a major triad while humming. Make sure to resonate the hum and feel the vibration in the front of your face. Keep your muscles loose and relaxed.

Humming Exercise Summary

Humming is a wonderful way to kick start your voice each day. You should hum a little first thing in the morning to warm your voice up. It's often a good gauge for the health of the voice. If the hum is immediately "buzzy," forward in the face, feels easy to produce and can be taken up and down through most of the range with little effort, then your voice is ready and primed for optimal singing. If the hum is unresponsive and hard to produce and the range is limited this may be an indication that you need more warm-ups that day. It could even mean your voice is in need of rest that day due to some other factors.

Lip Rolls

This is an excellent way to warm up and loosening the jaw, tongue, and lips. The Lip Roll or lip buzz exercise will warm up your lips and strengthen your diaphragm for singing. Your lips help shape the vowels as you sing so it is important to have them ready to roll!

Lip Roll Exercise

Lets go through the technique of doing a Lip Roll first then once you feel comfortable with it I will show you some pitch exercises to apply to this technique. Loosen your lips and just let them hang free as you blow air between them this time. If your lips are tight, place a finger at the corners of your mouth and gently push the corners toward your nose as you do the lip trill. The idea is to blow through their lips, causing them to vibrate rapidly. You should keep your lips tight enough together to create the right amount of resistance. When you have the lip trill flowing steady, start counting silently. Try to keep the lip roll going as long as you can. Make sure to take a deep breath and stay relaxed.

Lip Roll Pitch Exercises

Next you will apply the Lip Roll technique to pitches. By changing pitches while doing this exercise you will further expand the benefits.

Make sure to use the audio track demonstrations for this exercise to help guide you through these examples.

Exercise 1

Exercise 2

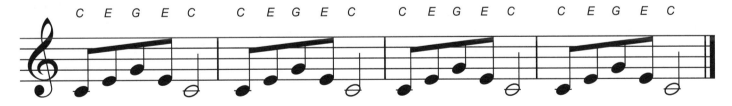

Slides & Sirens

This exercise is one of my favorites. It helps to coordinate your breathing and relaxing your face and it will help you warm up your high notes. When you sing high notes your vocal chords are stretching in a longer position. This will stretch them out and get them ready for you to belt those high notes with ease. When you sing this exercise you will make a sound very similar to a siren on a fire engine or police car. I remember when students sang this at the Rock House School of Music it always made other students chuckle a bit. So lets have some fun with this one and stretch those vocal chords out.

Slides & Sirens Exercise

Ok time to have some fun and sing this exercise. You will start on a comfortable low note and slide the note up to hit a high note in the upper range of your register. Use the "Ooo" sound when you sing this exercise. Start with a slow slide up and down and then you can work your way up to fast slides up and down. You need to open up your throat and allow the air to move forward, sliding up and down your pitches in a smooth, gentle transition. The siren sound should be loose and relaxed, don't push too hard or sing too loud. As you practice and get more comfortable with this exercises don't hold the high and low notes as long, make the up and down movement of your voice go fluidly up and down. This exercise will increase your pitch by stretching and not pushing to avoid tension. I know you will be making some obnoxious sounds but this is a great exercise so have some fun with it.

As I said earlier you will be making a sound similar to a siren so keep that in mind and try to simulate that sound. Make sure to listen to the audio example and demonstration for this exercise to hear how it should sound and to help guide you through this exercise effectively.

Tongue Trill Exercises

This is an excellent addition to the lip trill, especially if you are struggling with monitoring your controlled airflow, this exercise will help you to sustain your tone longer. The technique of this exercise is the same as "rolling an r" with your tongue.

The tongue trill uses the same principle in that you exhale and gently resist the flow in a controlled manner as the tongue vibrates with the passing air. Now I know that there are some people that just cannot roll their R's with the tongue. There can be a few reasons why; if you can curl your tongue in a tube like fashion but still can't roll the R's then you might have developed tension in the swallowing muscles that are up at the top of your jaw near your ears. So be patient because with the stretching exercises you may be able to teach yourself to roll your R's in time. If you can't get the R's to roll don't worry we will be doing other exercises in the course that will help achieve the same results. Everyone is different and we all have our unique abilities.

Tongue Trill Exercise

Now you will do the tongue trill using the same two patterns you used in the Humming Exercises. Keep the sound of the trill above your cheeks and not falling back in your throat. Also think down as you hit the higher notes to keep your technique proper, if you don't you will be reaching for the higher notes and lose the technique you need for the tongue trills.

Make sure to listen to the audio example and demonstration to help guide you through this exercise.

Exercise 1

Exercise 2

Tongue Trill "O" Shape Siren Exercise

Shape your lips in an "O" shape and try the tongue trill exercise, start with a comfortable lower pitch and slide up to a high note and back down. By keeping your lips in the "O" shape you get a more controlled and relaxed facial position. If you do this in a more open mouth position make sure not to tighten up especially in the back of your tongue. So you are combining the Siren Slide exercise with the Tongue Trill in this exercise.

Repetition is the Mother of Skill

The real key to strengthening you voice is singing as much as you can. But in order to accomplish this you need to build up your singing stamina and create good singing habits. These exercises are a great way to get started. Make sure you commit time every day to practice these exercises and you will begin to see results quickly. One of my favorite sayings is "Repetition is the mother of skill" practice these everyday and you will see results!

Chapter 7
Ear Training for Singers

To become a great singer you need to train your ear so you can hear tones more effectively, I tell my students that you have to hear the notes before you can sing them. Part of that is perception the other part is actually hearing the notes. You must make ear training a vital part of all of your singing practice.

Here are some great ear training exercises you should be doing to help you develop your musical ear and become a better singer.

Be an Active Listener

There is a difference between hearing music and "Listening to Music." Most people hear music as one big whole, so when they listen to the music they don't hear specific things within the music like the bass drum or the piano or guitar. It just sounds like one chunk of music to them. Here is the exercise I want you to do.

Exercise

Get one of your favorite songs to listen to. As the song is playing I want you to listen specifically for an instrument or musical sound. You need to target these and try to block out the rest of the songs instruments. It is not easy at first so be patient and practice this often. Here is what I want you to listen for:

1. **The Bass Drum** – This is a low thumping drum sound and it falls often on the 1 and 3 beats of a song. So if you count 1 – 2 – 3 – 4 along with the song listen close on 1 and 3 and see if it is there.

2. **The Snare Drum** – This is a higher pitched rattle sounding drum. It usually counters back and forth with the bass drum to create the rhythm groove for the song. So if the bass drum is sounding on the 1 and 3 the snare will often sound on the 2 and 4 beats. The reason I wanted you to listen specifically for these two drums first is because this creates the rhythm for the song and it will help you to stay in time as you sing.

3. **The Bass Guitar** – If you haven't heard a bass guitar before it is the low-pitched sound in the song. The reason this instrument is important is because it usually outlines the song chord structure. The bass guitar usually follows the chord progression. If you are listening to the song on something that has EQ where you can turn the bass up or treble down, you should do this because it will make the bass guitar stand out in the track.

4. **Guitar** – This can be electric or acoustic guitar. They each have a distinct sound. The guitar plays the chords of the song. The chords that form a song will also contain the notes that you will use to sing harmonies. The better you can hear these notes the easier it will be to sing harmonies.

5. **Piano** – In the same fashion as the guitar the piano will have the chord structure for the song and contain the notes you can use for harmonies.

Though it's simple this truly is one of the best ways to grow your musical ear. It will benefit your musical memory, your discernment of pitch, your appreciation of timbre, your awareness of harmony, and so much more.

Pitch Training and Singing in Tune

Singing in tune is vital for being a good singer and pleasing listeners with your voice. You probably don't need to be reminded of the last time you heard someone singing out of tune and instinctively cringed in discomfort! Or perhaps you've even had people tell you that you're "off-key" or "out of tune" yourself? Singing on key is something you NEED to be good at and I'll give you a few simple exercises to help you train. Being able to sing in tune depends 100% on being able to hear in tune. That means using your ears to judge whether notes are too high or too low. Now lets work on your first exercise.

Exercise

You will need an instrument to do this exercise and a guitar or piano will work best. On the instrument you choose, play random single notes in the middle voice register. The middle register on a piano is from one octave higher to one octave lower from the middle C note. Play the note and let it ring and then sing the notes pitch using the "La" sound. Don't swoop up to the note sing it right to the pitch. As you get better at this exercise make big jumps in pitch from high to low this will make it more challenging. You can also go faster from note to note as you get better at singing the notes in the exercise. Pitch ear training is the process of refining your ability to judge pitches in music. Spend some time training your ears for pitch and your voice will rapidly improve. The next exercise you will work on for pitch training will be singing to specific intervals.

Relative Pitch Leaps

Relative pitch is your ability to judge how far apart notes are from each other. These are also called intervals (the distance between two notes) you will need to have your pitch skills from the previous exercise developed to help in this exercise although it is a different skill. Relative pitch for singers is about knowing how far apart two notes are when you need to transition from one to the other. This could be big leaps such as an octave or smaller intervals between notes in a melody. Either way you need to instinctively understand these distances by ear. Here is your exercise to help you develop relative pitch.

Exercise

You will start by singing middle C and then sing different intervals up from that C note. What you need to focus on is the distance each interval is from middle C again using the "La" sound. You need to hear the note and its relation to the starting note middle C. This will be your start to ear training as well.

- Play middle C and then the very next note D. Sing these notes along as you play them.
- Play C and then the E note two keys up and sing along.
- Play C and then F and sing along.
- Play C and then G and sing along
- Play C and then A and sing along.
- Play C and then B and sing along.
- Play C and then C an octave higher and sing along.

As you do this exercise you are singing all the intervals of the C major scale. Ear training for intervals will help you refine your sense of relative pitch. This will in turn make it much easier for you to judge those vocal leaps accurately and sing better. It will also help you understand harmony.

Summary

Spending time to work on perfecting your pitch and ability to hear notes will make you a better singer, it is a fact! As you spend time singing make sure you devote time to ear training too. Your technical ability as a singer depends heavily on the ears you are equipped with. Develop a trained ear and you will become more musical, more proficient and more confident as a singer, I promise this to you.

Chapter 8
Proper Technique to Get Started

Ok its time to start singing. I will guide you through a series of vocal exercises that will help you train your voice. You need to think about hitting the pitches sharply and concentrate on your tone. Here are a few last minute tips to keep on mind as you start these exercises.

Remember to Open Your Mouth as You Sing

I know this may sound simple and should be common sense but I can't tell you how many times I had to tell a student "Open Your mouth!" When most people start singing they need to be reminded that to create a full vocal sound you need to open your mouth. So don't be afraid to show off those pearly whites. Open your mouth to project your sound. This is the most important thing singers need to know. There are many benefits of opening wide when you sing but the main one is: Vocal Tones Can Only be Projected When The Mouth is Generously Opened.

Yawn to Open the Back of your Throat

In singing, backspace refers to the space in the back of the mouth as well as your throat. Opening your throat is something all singers must learn to do as early as possible. Yawn with your lips closed, this should create the open space you need while singing. Feel the open space you've created in the back of your mouth and throat. Keep this and the yawn exercises we worked on previously in mind as you start these exercises to open your throat wide.

How to Gauge your Open Mouth Spacing

Here's a tip to help you open your mouth wider, it's simple and it works. Wash and dry your hands before you do the following:

- Locate the first and second finger on either your right or left hand.
- Place these two fingers on top of each other just inside your mouth between your front upper and lower teeth.
- Keep your jaw relaxed.
- This is about how much space you will need for singing.
- Now with the fingers still in your mouth sing ahhh on a comfortable pitch. Avoid singing too high or too low.
- Hold the ahhh sound for the count of 8.
- Repeat this exercise but this time remove the fingers from your mouth on the count of two, still sustaining the ahhh sound.

It's natural to feel uncomfortable in the beginning especially if you normally sing with a small mouth opening. Don't worry about it. Keep practicing and before you know it singing this way will feel normal.

Drop Your Jaw to Project While Singing

The following exercise is one that I teach my vocal students regardless of the level of expertise they claim to have:

- To feel the space inside your mouth pretend that you have an egg in the back of your mouth.
- When air is moved through your mouth the "egg" space remains open.
- Sing a part of your favorite song finding the openness of the yawn and imagining the egg space in the back of your throat.

Great singing is all about naturally feeling the mechanics of the voice working its magic. Only when you are aware are you able to bring about change. Study the way you sound and how your body feels as you sing. This is especially important when you first learn to sing and working on the following vocal exercises.

You were born with the tools needed to develop a great voice. These tools are available to you right now. You simply need to learn how to use them properly. So lets get started!

Chapter 9
Lets Start Singing – Beginner Vocal Exercises

The first exercises are simple ones to get you started on track and concentrating on note pitches. You must try to hit each notes pitch without swooping up to the note. Think of singing each note as shooting a dark at a specific pitch. Focus on the pitch you want to sing for each note. Make sure to take a deep breath before you sing and don't let your breath out quickly. Stand tall and keep good posture because this will help you to support each note properly.

Sing Up Three Notes
Do - Re - Me

Do – Re – Me represent the first three notes of a major scale. The accompanying audio track starts on middle C and goes up two full octaves giving you a good starting point for your vocal range.

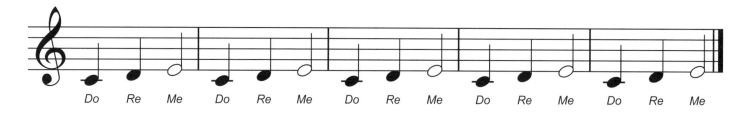

Sing Up & Down Three Notes
Do – Re – Me / Me – Re – Do

In this exercise you will sing up and down the first three notes of the major scale. I know this seems simple but it is important to learn the basics before getting into more difficult exercises.

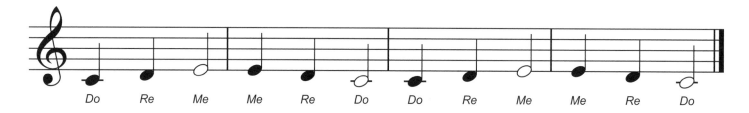

Up Down & All Around
Do – Re – Me / Me – Re – Do / Do – Me – Re / Re – Me – Do

In this exercise you ascend and descend in 1 & 2 step intervals. An interval is the distance between two notes. You will start singing in larger intervals as we progress through the course.

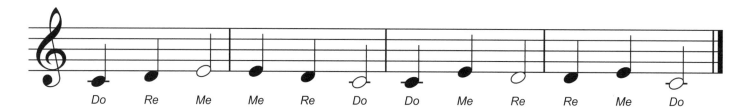

Five Note Scale Ascend

Now you will sing a series of exercises using a 5 - note ascending scale pattern. These notes are the first five notes of the major scale. The thing you need to concentrate on here is how you start with a consonant and then shape your mouth for the vowel. The following are the sounds you will use and a description of how you should shape your mouth for each vowel. We will be working more thoroughly on vowels, mouth shape and proper pronunciations in the next chapter.

Exercise 1 – Mah – Mah – Mah – Mah – Mah

Start with your lips together and then open your mouth in a long shape for each "Ma" sound.

Exercise 2 – Bee – Bee – Bee – Bee – Bee

For the "Be" sound, start with your lips together then open your mouth wide, only this time open in a wide shape left to right.

Exercise 3 – Hee – Hee – Hee – Hee – Hee

For the "He" sound, start with your mouth slightly open and keep your tongue low in your mouth against the back of your bottom teeth.

Exercise 4 – Tee – Tee – Tee – Tee – Tee

To sing the "Te" sound your tongue plays a big role. Find a comfortable spot to place your tongue touching your front teeth and the top of your mouth.

Exercise 5 – Nah – No – Mee – Gee – Mah

When singing these sounds your mouth will be taking many different shapes. Keep your mouth open and shaped as you pronounce the vowel in each.

Five Note Descending Scale

Next you will do a series of exercises singing down or descending the major scale. Many singers swoop up to the first note when singing in descending exercises which has a lot to do with perception; if you visualize that you are coming down to the first note instead of seeing it as grabbing up to the note you will hit the note precisely with ease. You will use the same five sound pronunciation words that you used ascending as follows.

Exercise 1 – Mah – Mah – Mah – Mah – Mah

Start with your lips together and then open your mouth in a long shape for each "Ma" sound.

Exercise 2 – Bee – Bee – Bee – Bee – Bee

For the "Be" sound, start with your lips together then open your mouth wide, only this time open in a wide shape left to right.

Exercise 3 – Hee – Hee – Hee – Hee – Hee

For the "He" sound, start with your mouth slightly open and keep your tongue low in your mouth against the back of your bottom teeth.

Exercise 4 – Tee – Tee – Tee – Tee – Tee

To sing the "Te" sound your tongue plays a big role. Find a comfortable spot to place your tongue touching your front teeth and the top of your mouth.

Exercise 5 – Nah – No – Mee – Gee – Mah

When singing these sounds in a row your mouth will be taking many different shapes. Keep your mouth open and shaped as you pronounce the vowel in each.

Chapter 10
Vocal Expression - Singing the Vowels

In this chapter you will learn to sing the vowels. Singing the vowels properly will give your voice distinction and power. By learning how to shape your mouth and sound each vowel correctly you will also have better diction, sing clear and your audience will be able to notice the difference. Lets dive into this now!

Good Articulation Starts with Singing the Vowels

As a singer YOU are the instrument and your entire body is involved in creating your unique sound. When singing you need to combine and control many parts of the body in order to sing well. One of the most important techniques to master is proper singing of the primary vowels. These are the primary vowel pronunciations:

Ah Eh Ee Oh Oo

The Five Pure Primary Vowels Used in Singing

Every vowel should be enunciated with your tongue forward in the mouth, tucked neatly behind your bottom teeth. The back of the tongue should be kept away from the throat to keep the sound nice and clear. Always keep the tongue relaxed and free from tension when singing.

Before you use these vowel sounds in an exercise I want you to get familiar with them. Speak each of the vowel sounds below. Once you feel comfortable speaking the vowels sounds sing them all in a comfortable singing pitch:

- Ah – as in Father
- Eh – as in Pet
- Ee – as in Meet
- Oh – as in Dome
- Oo – as in Blue

Here are the specific ways you should sing each vowel sound:

Ah – To sing this vowel sound, position your mouth wide open in an oval shape. Don't tense the jaw or tongue. It is crucial to keep these areas as relaxed as possible. This will give you a smooth and rich tone without tension

Eh – To sing this vowel sound, place your lips in such a way that you are just beginning a smile. Keep the tongue very relaxed in the bed of the mouth with the tip resting lightly against the bottom front teeth

Ee – To sing this vowel sound, place your tongue flat resting against the bottom front teeth. The lips are in a relaxed in a slight "smile" position. The slight rise of the cheeks will pull the lips into perfect position to sing this vowel

Oh – To sing this vowel sound, its fairly simple you shape your lips in an actual "O" shape.

Oo – To sing this vowel sound, think of puckering up to give a kiss but leave a space in the middle open. I tell students to think like they are pushing their lips out away from the face.

As you can probably see by trying these 5 vowel sounds, it's important to get proper formation of the mouth including the jaw and cheeks. Keep your lips relaxed as you position them for each vowel. If you have too much tension in the lip area you will create more tension in the tone, which will affect the sound of your voice. You must shape the vowel within the word clearly and this will improve your overall singing ability.

Let me give you an example, sing the word "father". The sound of "ah" requires a dropped jaw. If the jaw is tense and doesn't drop enough, the word "father" may sound like "further" to the listener. You need to pay attention and hear when you are doing this and correct yourself.

You want your fans to understand the words you are singing especially if you are writing your own music. If you put deep thought into creating lyrics you want your listeners to hear them clearly and hopefully sing along. So to become a great all around artist and performer you must articulate your words as you sing.

Many of my students think I'm crazy when I tell them they are singing the vowels incorrectly. They think that when singing words the vowels are pronounced the same way as when they speak.

There are 26 letters in the alphabet but there are only 5 primary vowels. These 5 vowels when executed properly in singing will create a full tone resulting in a clear distinct sound unique to only you!

Singing the Primary Vowel Sounds
Exercise 1

Now you will sing all 5 vowel sounds all on a single pitch and then ascend up the scale one note at a time using the audio backing track. If you just casually speak the words for this exercise your lips probably would be narrow and closed. But when you sing this exercise your mouth should be open and rounder. Keep in mind the mouth shapes for the primary vowel sounds you just learned because these are the pronunciations you will be singing.

Exercise 2

In this exercise you will make the five primary vowel sounds only with the letter M before each. This will require you closing your lips before pronouncing each sound. You will go up the scale singing each on the same note.

Ma Meh Me Mo Moo   Ma Meh Me Mo Moo

Ma Meh Me Mo Moo   Ma Meh Me Mo Moo

Have Some Fun with the Vowels

Here is an exercise to help you pronounce the vowels correctly and distinctly. Use the pronunciations to the right for the bold underlined words in each sentence.

- **I** am happy **I'm here**.. **AH – ee......AH – eem....HEE – r**

- **I** love to play guitar. .... **AH – ee**

- **I** sing with **my** friends. .... **AH – ee......MAH – ee**

- The pleasure is **mine**. .... **MAH – een**

- It's important to know **our vowels**. .... **AH – oor......VAH – ools**

- You should **know how** to ride a bike. .... **KNOOH – oo......HAH – oo**

- **I** need **space** to move. .... **AH – ee......SPEH – eece**

Chapter 11
Vocal Exercises Level 1

You will start your first complete vocal exercise routine now. There are 15 exercises in this vocal workout routine. Sing each of these exercises repetitively and make sure to use the audio backing tracks that correspond with each. The backing tracks go up one full octave and should challenge your range. I've included a male and female example for each but you can use either depending on your range and how much you want to push your range lower or higher.

1 – Me Mo My

The first vocal exercise is a three-note major scale ascending and descending pattern. I call it the 1 – 2 – 3 – 2 – 1 pattern. Your mouth shape will change for each vowel sound as you learned in the vowels section in this course. Use the accompanying backing track to sing the exercise.

Sing the following vocal sounds while practicing this exercise:

1.   Me – Me – Me – Me – Me
2.   Mo – Mo – Mo – Mo – Mo
3.   My – My – My – My - My

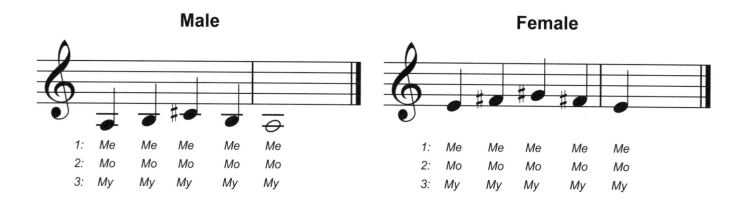

Backing Tracks

The following exercises require you to use the audio backing tracks to sing along with. To practice with these backing tracks follow along as the exercises goes higher or lower until you are not able to match the pitch. You must push yourself everyday to expand your range and broaden your vocal horizons. If the track is too low or high for your starting vocal range you may need to start a few intervals up as the exercise progresses. You can download the backing tracks and play them with any device that is convenient for you in your practice area. Any time there is a backing track that you should be singing along with you will see the backing track icon at the beginning of the exercise.

2 – The Five Note Scale Descend

In this vocal exercise you will descend down 5 notes of a major scale. Even though you are singing the first note at the highest pitch I want you to think as if you are going down to the first note not reaching up to the note. This is part of the perception that will help you hit higher notes with ease. I call this exercise the 5 – 4 – 3 – 2 – 1 pattern.

Sing the following vocal sounds while practicing this exercise:

1.   La   La   La   La   La
2.   Me   Me   Me   Me   Me

Male   **Female**

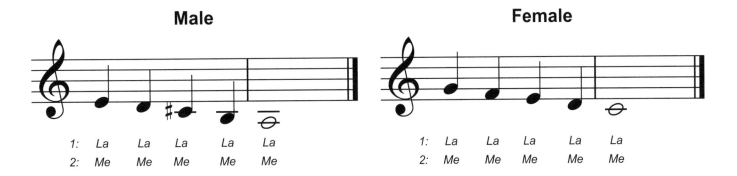

| 1: | La | La | La | La | La |
| 2: | Me | Me | Me | Me | Me |

3 – The Major Scale 5th Dip

In this exercise you will sing a scale pattern and drop from the 5th to root note at the end. Singing intervals such as this will help you to train your voice to sing melodies that are more complex with precision. I call this exercise the 5 – 4 – 3 – 4 – 5 – 1.

Sing the following vocal sounds while practicing this exercise:

We – Ah – We – Ah – Wee – Ahh

Male   **Female**

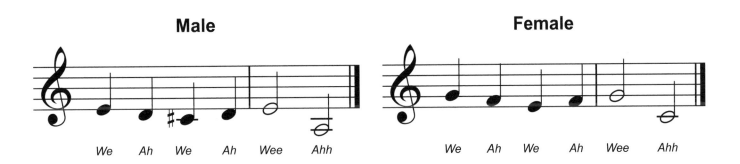

We   Ah   We   Ah   Wee   Ahh

4 – Descending 4 - 3

This exercise is a descending major scale pattern in a sequence of 4 and 3. The two vowel sounds you will need to shape your mouth for are E and Ah. Notice the different placement you will need with the mouth and tongue when starting on the letter M in relation to the letter L. With the letter M your lips close between each pronunciation but with the letter L you keep an open position. The pattern within the scale this exercise follows is 5- -4 – 3 – 2 – 3 – 2 – 1.

Sing the following vocal sounds while practicing this exercise:

1.   **Me – Ma – Me – Ma – Me – Ma – Me**
2.   **Lee – La – Lee – La – Lee – La – Lee**

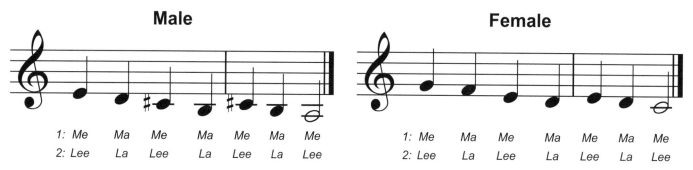

5 – Octave Slide & Major Scale Descend

An octave is a large interval to sing. If you don't have music theory knowledge an octave is going up 8 scale degrees to the same note at a higher pitch. In this exercise you will start with an octave slide then descend down every degree of the major scale back to your starting note. Sing the E sound for all notes in the exercise.

Sing the following vocal sounds while practicing this exercise:

EE – EE – E – E – E – E – E – E – E – E

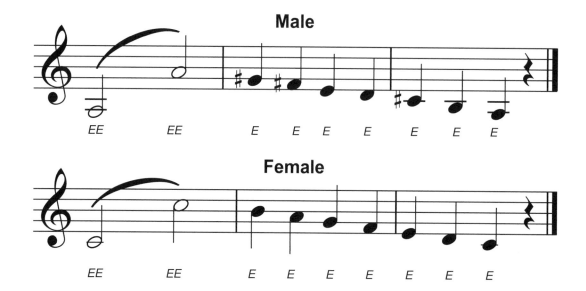

6 – Staccato Run

Staccato by definition mean short & detached and staccato is a technique you will use in singing often. Staccato can help you emphasize a note by cutting it short and adding volume as well. Make sure you support the staccato note in your abdomen; you can hold your hand on the stomach to make sure you feel the support.

Sing the following vocal sounds while practicing this exercise:

Me – Ya | Me – Ya | Me – Ya – Ah – Ah – Ah

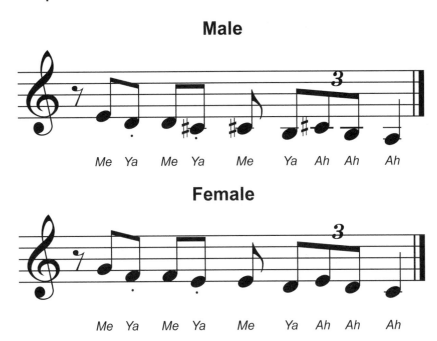

7 – Down & Up the Vowels

As you learned previously in this course the vowels are very important to sing properly and accurately. In this exercise you will sing down-up-down the first five notes of the major scale using A – E – I – O. Make sure you shape your mouth in the proper shape for each vowel you sing.

Sing the following vocal sounds while practicing this exercise:

A – A – A – A – E – E – E – E – I – I – I – I – O

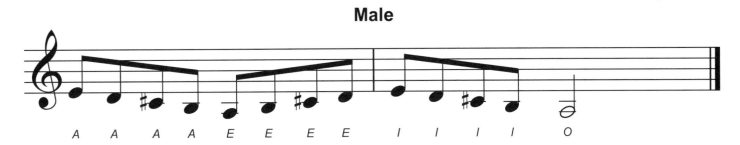

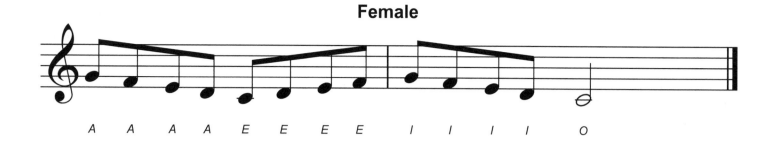

A   A   A   A   E   E   E   E   I   I   I   I   O

8 – Minor Vowels Runs

For this exercise you will use the same basic techniques from the previous exercise only this time you will be singing down & up the minor scale. Minor scales give your singing a darker sad feel. You will use minor and major scales when you sing and songs to create emotion in your singing.

Sing the following vocal sounds while practicing this exercise:

A – A – A – A – E – E – E – E – I – I – I – I – O

Male

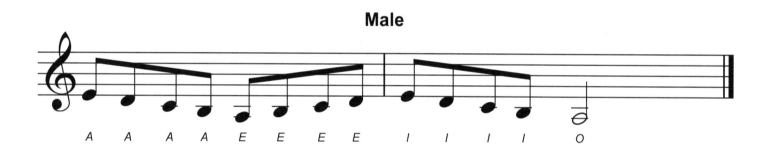

A   A   A   A   E   E   E   E   I   I   I   I   O

Female

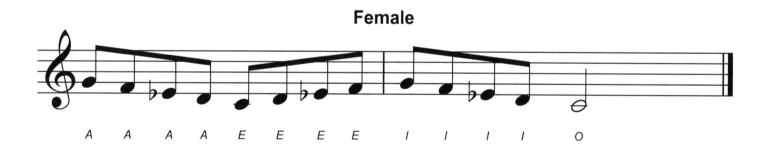

A   A   A   A   E   E   E   E   I   I   I   I   O

9 – Major Arpeggio Yah Yah Yah

An arpeggio is the notes of a chord sounded separately. The major arpeggio you will sing for this exercise contains the 1st, 3rd and 5th degrees of the major scale. For this exercise you will sing the Yah sound for each note and I want you to not hold back. Belt out each note with power and make sure to support each note from your mid-section.

Sing the following vocal sounds while practicing this exercise:

Yah – Yah – Yah – Yah – Yah – Yah – Yah

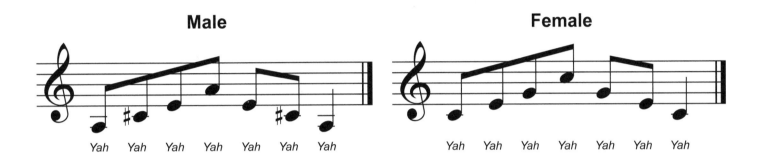

10 – Yeah – Yeah – Yeah

You will sing the same arpeggios as you did in the previous exercise only this time you will sing the arpeggio with "Yeah." Sing the Yeah with attitude as if you were saying, "Yeah that's right!"

Sing the following vocal sounds while practicing this exercise:

Yeah – Yeah – Yeah – Yeah – Yeah – Yeah – Yeah

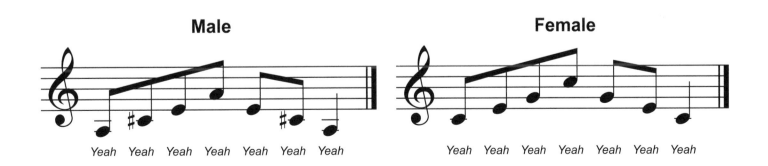

11 – Be Za Descending Staccato

Here is another staccato exercise to help you learn to sing staccato. Make sure you open your mouth to the appropriate shape for each vowel.

Sing the following vocal sounds while practicing this exercise:

Be – Za | Be – Za | Be – Za | Be – Za |

Male

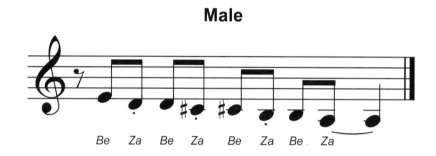

Be   Za   Be   Za   Be   Za   Be   Za

Female

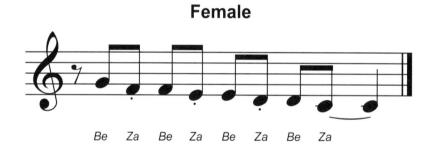

Be   Za   Be   Za   Be   Za   Be   Za

12 – Chromatic Singing

Singing chromatic means to sing in half step intervals. A half step is the smallest interval in music. On a piano it is from any key to the very next key black or white, on a guitar it is from any fret to the very next fret. In this exercise you are going to sing up a series of half step intervals using two different sounds "E" and "OO." I want you to take a deep breath in and control your breathing to last the whole way up the scale and then take another deep breath to come down the scale.

Sing the following vocal sounds while practicing this exercise:

Ascending and Descending

1. E   E   E   E   E   E   E   E
2. OO – OO – OO – OO – OO – OO – OO - OO

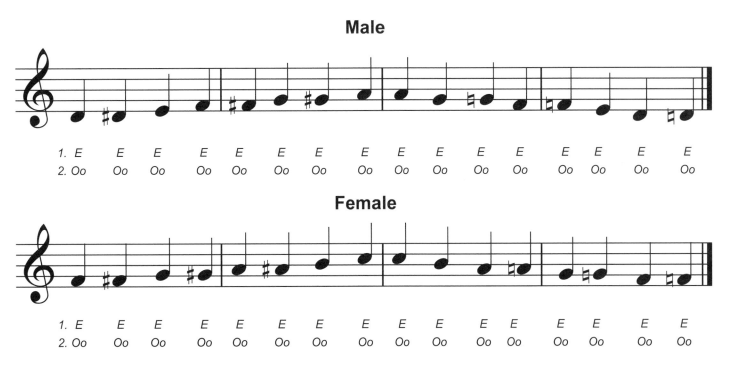

1. E   E   E   E   E   E   E   E   E   E   E   E   E   E   E   E
2. Oo Oo Oo Oo Oo Oo Oo Oo Oo Oo Oo Oo Oo Oo Oo Oo

Female

1. E   E   E   E   E   E   E   E   E   E   E   E   E   E   E   E
2. Oo Oo Oo Oo Oo Oo Oo Oo Oo Oo Oo Oo Oo Oo Oo Oo

13 – 5th Slide Down Adding the Minor 3rd

For this exercise you will be doing a 5th slide, which means you start on the 5th degree of the scale sand then slide down to the root note. The third time you will be adding a minor 3rd into the slide so it will be 5th – minor 3rd, root. There will be two variations to this exercise using "Lee – Lou" and "Ma – Me."

Sing the following vocal sounds while practicing this exercise:

1. Lee Lou Lee Lou Lee E   Lou
2. Ma   Me   Ma   Me   Ma   Ah   Me

Male

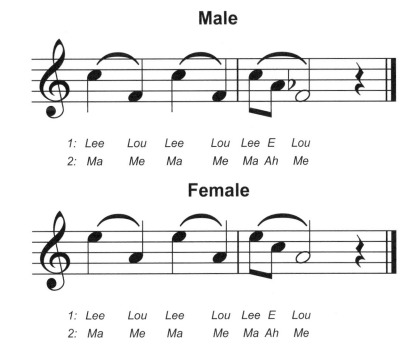

1: Lee   Lou   Lee   Lou Lee E Lou
2: Ma   Me   Ma   Me   Ma Ah Me

Female

1: Lee   Lou   Lee   Lou Lee E Lou
2: Ma   Me   Ma   Me   Ma Ah Me

14 – Vocal Riff

Just like a guitar player plays a riff in a lead you can sing riffs as well. These require more coordination and control. This exercise will help you to gain the control you need to sing riffs and runs. It is a quick run so you need to focus on the notes and hit them right on and not make it too slurry. You will use the "E" sound for the first four notes and then "La" for the last part of the riff.

Sing the following vocal sounds while practicing this exercise:

E – E – E – E – La – La – La– La – La – La – La

Male

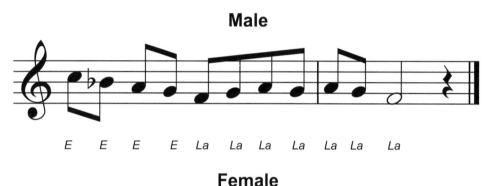

Female

15 – The Chromatic Slide

This exercise will help you in your transition from your full voice to head voice or falsetto. You will start with an octave slide up and then sing a chromatic riff at the end. Use the "E" sound as you sing this exercise along with the audio track.

Sing the following vocal sounds while practicing this exercise:

E / E – E – E – E – E

Male

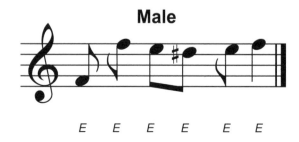

Female

Chapter 12
Intervals

In music you have timing and this refers to the duration you hold a note when you sing and you have pitch which is how low or high you sing the note. An interval describes the pitch by how large or small the distance is between the two notes. When you sing you will be jumping from note to note going higher and lower and how far up and down to go changes the interval. Below you will see the notation for all the intervals and their names. If you can play an instrument play each of the intervals and start to hear the sound they create. I have included a backing track if you don't play an instrument so you can hear how they sound as well before you sing them.

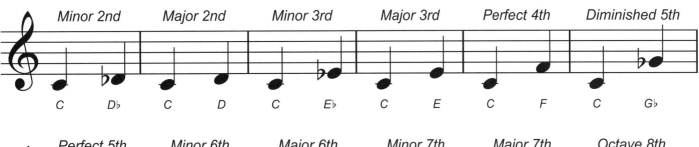

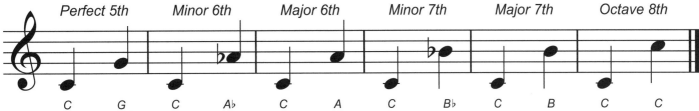

Singing the Intervals

Now its time to sing each interval. On the audio track you will hear each interval and then it will just have the root and you must sing the interval on your own. Repetition is the mother of skill for learning to sing the intervals, so sing them repetitively until it becomes natural.

When singing these intervals use any of the vowel sounds you learned in the Singing the Vowels lesson:

Ah – Eh – Ee – Oh – Oo

Minor Second

The Minor 2nd interval is the smallest interval being just a half step. It is not used in harmonies often because it is too close to the root note but it is a good exercise to help you learn to sing a half step interval.

Major Second

A Major 2nd interval is a whole step. The Major 2nd is not used often in harmonies, the Major 2nd is more commonly used when sung an octave higher as a ninth in relationship to the root note. Singing whole steps will help you to train your voice, you will sing whole notes in melodies often.

Male   **Female**

Minor Third

The Minor 3rd interval is used in harmonies and because it is a minor interval it creates a sad tone when sung along with the root note. You will hear this as you sing the exercise.

Male   **Female**

Major Third

The Major 3rd harmony is probably the most used harmony note in all singing. It creates a happy sound when sung along with the root note; you will hear this when you sing the exercise. Get the sound of this harmony in your ears because you will sing this harmony often as you develop as a lead singer.

Male   **Female**

Perfect Fourth

The perfect 4th interval is a dissonant interval. A dissonant interval is one that has tension; it doesn't feel as natural as say a 3rd or a 5th interval. This doesn't mean it is not a good note to use as a harmony, in fact if used in the right spot in a song it can be very effective. Music is tension and release so you need times within a song that tension builds to make the other parts sound more effective.

Diminished Fifth

The diminished fifth is often called a tri-tone in modern tonal theory, but functionally and in notation it can only resolve inwards as a diminished fifth. It is an interval composed of three adjacent whole steps. The Diminished 5th has the most tension of all the intervals. To an untrained ear it can even sound bad. Again when you want to create tension you can use this interval. You may be surprised to find out that many metal bands use the Diminished 5th in their guitar rhythms in songs.

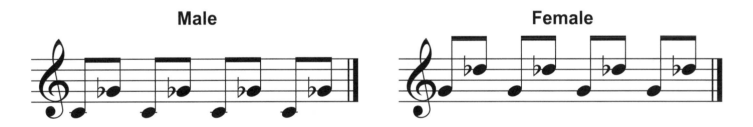

Perfect Fifth

The perfect 5th interval is probably the most important interval in music. The 5th and root are in the chord structure of almost every chord. In rock music many song use what is called "Power Chords" or 5 chords and these chords use only the root and 5th degrees. The 3rd and 5th intervals are by far the most used in singing harmonies. The 5th interval is a consonant interval, which means it is very pleasing to hear.

Minor Sixth

The minor 6th interval while not as popular as the 3rd and 5th can be used in harmonies but more importantly it is used in singing melodies often. You need to have all these intervals in your singing arsenal to be able to create your own melodies as well.

Major Sixth

Again as with the minor 6th the major 6th interval is not as popular as the 3rd and 5th but it is used in singing melodies often. The 6th interval is a dissonant interval. Get familiar with its sound you will be singing this interval in many melodies.

Minor Seventh

The minor 7th interval is another common interval used in creating melodies in songs. You can hear its minor tone when you hear it against the root note.

Major Seventh

The major 7th interval is the interval right before the octave. It is 11 half steps up a scale. The major 7th interval is therefore and very big jump up from the root if you are singing it.

The Octave

The octave interval is a very difficult interval to sing because it is a large jump from the root. It is the same pitch letter name for both notes so it makes it a bit easier to hit the proper pitch.

Assess Your Voice

When you first started this course I asked you to assess your voice to see what your highest and lowest notes you could sing were and asked you to record a song you felt comfortable singing. Now it's time to check and see your progress.

1. *Use an instrument to check your range and see what the lowest and highest notes you can sing are. Compare this to when you first started the course and hopefully you have seen this expand.*

2. *Record the same song you sang at the beginning of the course. As you start to have better technique you should also see an improvement in the tone and quality of your voice.*

It is important to continuously asses your progress and analyze your strengths and weaknesses to become the best singer you can be.

Chapter 13
Vocal Techniques

The Vocal Lift… Nail Those High Notes! Ave Maria

All singers want to hit those soaring high notes with ease. With repetitive practice with the vocal exercises in this course you will be able to expand your range both higher and lower but there is also some techniques that can help you sing these high notes more effectively. The Vocal Lift is a technique that you can use that will help you get a new perspective on these high notes and visualize them in a new effective way and the end result will be you singing high notes without tensing up your vocal track and straining your voice. With the Vocal Lift you take the note right before the high note and visualize this as the highest note to put you in position to sing the high note with ease. This technique helps you feel as though you are coming down in pitch to sing the high note and this perception helps you sing the note without straining and reaching for it. You need to picture your notes below you. Think down when you go up. You can literally move down (bend your knees) when you sing up. Think down when going up, and up when going down and you will hit your notes with ease.

Exercise

In this exercise visualize the Ma or the 2nd to the highest note as the highest note and sing down to the highest pitch note on Re. When I am teaching this to students I even use my hand to help students visualize this by raising my hand higher on Ma and lowering it when they sing the Re. You should try using your hand in this fashion as well it will help you to get the perception you need to use this technique most effectively.

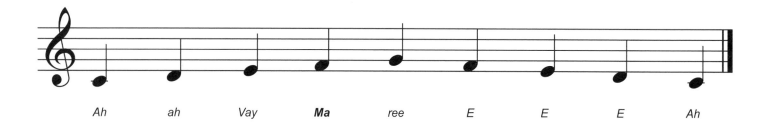

| Ah | ah | Vay | **Ma** | ree | E | E | E | Ah |

The Straw Technique

The Straw Technique will help you recover your voice from strain and fatigue. It is also a great exercise to warm up your voice and get your vocal folds ready to rock! Every singer needs to get their voice rejuvenated and hitting on all cylinders to sing at your optimum level.

What you will need to execute this exercise is two sipping straws. These are the thin plastic straws not those big fat ones. You will be singing through these straws, I know it sounds strange but believe me there is a method to my madness. When you sing through the straws it will create pressure in the back of the throat or the pharynx. When you put pressure on the back of the throat you stretch open the vocal cavity this allows the vocal chords (folds) to lengthen and stretch out. Vocal folds function best when they are thin and lean so they can close more effectively. By singing into the straws this is actually stretching the vocal chords and getting them ready to sing at peak performance.

If you find that you get raspy after singing it is a sign that you are using too much vocal cord mass and the result is the thickening of the vocal chords. When vocal folds become thicker they also become less vibrant. This exercise will help you get those vocal folds back in shape.

Take the straws and put them in the middle of your lips and close your lips around them. You will be singing through the straws using the exercises in this lesson.

As you are singing the exercise you will notice that it isn't easy to get a lot of sound out. Make sure not to let air escape through your nose. If you have trouble not letting the air out through your nose you can try pinching the nose closed while singing. To check if you are executing the technique properly you can put you finger at the end of the straw while you are singing and this should mute the sound completely. Make sure to keep your tongue relaxed. You will not get a lot of sound out because most of the sound will be inside your mouth.

As you get better at applying the technique you may feel vibrations inside your head while singing, this means that your vocal folds are thinning out and vibrating on the edges and producing more head voice.

Below are two exercises that you will sing through the straws. Following the technique that I described in this lesson.

Exercise 1

Exercise 2

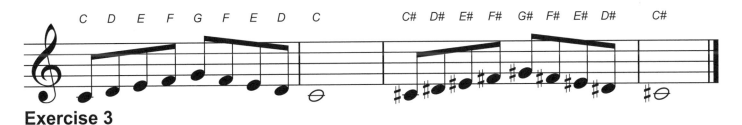

Exercise 3

Next you will sing a song through the straws. I recommend a very easy song such as Amazing Grace or even Happy Birthday. But you can sing any song you would like.

Open Throat Singing

Focused Tone and Open Throat

Open throat singing is a technique where space is increased in the back of the throat and the vocal folds are retracted to increase space in the resonating section in the vocal tract. This involves raising the soft palate and lowering the larynx and getting the lips, tongue and jaw relaxed and in ideal position to sing. This technique helps singers relax the vocal region and avoid constriction of the throat that can cause harm to the voice.

When you are able to achieve the "Open Throat" singing technique you will sing and resonate a higher sound quality and a vibrant warm tone. It helps you produce balance and consistency in your singing and helps you avoid sounding thin or shrill. Here is how to think of it, if you go into a tiny room or even a closet and sing the sound will be small. But, in contrast if you went into a big room with wood wall and ceiling maybe like a church and started singing you would get a full resonating sound. The same thing goes for your throat, if it is tight and constricted you will sound thin and small, but if you create an open space and give your singing room to resonate you will create a big full singing tone.

The "Open Throat" sound is generated when the following vocal actions take place: your larynx lowers automatically when you take a breath in and the soft palate raises at the same time. And because singing is more demanding then just speaking you need to inhale deeper and use more energy and force.

When people sing in a closed voice or throat they usually lose the balance of the register they are singing, the chest register gets too high and the upper register starts sounding very thin. Intonation becomes harder to achieve because the larynx is too high and soft palate too low. It is important to set a solid foundation to support your singing to sing at your highest potential.

While singing with an open throat will help you achieve a better singing quality it is not the cure for all singing problems but a great technique to get familiar with to expand your vocal horizons.

There are many teachers that try to explain the Open Throat technique but fail in the application. One common mistake is confusing Open Mouth with Open Throat. In fact a jaw dropped too low actually places tension on the larynx lowers the soft palate and stops the closure of the vocal folds which is completely opposite of the desired results.

Applying the Open Throat Technique

Lets get into how to sing open throat now. Get into your singers stance and relax your body. You are going to sing an "Ah" sound and as you do this hold a happy expression on your face, not a full-blown smile. Do this by gently raising your cheeks with the muscles that wrap around the sides of your mouth. These are the same ones that lift the corners of your mouth when you smile. You may feel your facial muscles quivering or twitching at first but with repetition it will feel more natural as your muscles get stronger. With most people the facial muscles tend to pull down while singing you need to train yourself to raise the muscles.

Next I want you to 'inhale' a soft, quiet 'k' sound. Try to imagine drinking in the breath or inhaling the breath. This technique lifts the soft palate further, separating it from the tongue, and lowers the larynx as you inhale. Make sure not to inhale a loud or forced 'k' sound it will not create the proper technique.

The best part about this method of achieving an open throat is how effortless and natural it is for the singer. The soft plate naturally rises and the larynx automatically lowers during inhalation, and since you are forming and natural facial posture it directly affects the position of the soft palate, raising it slightly.

The thing you must work on is maintaining the open position of the vocal tract while you sing entire phrases and don't allow tension or constriction enter the throat.

Exercise - Open it up "uh"

In this exercise you will use the neutral vowel "uh" to help train you to sing in open throat and get your throat muscles stronger to maintain open throat singing through entire phrases. This technique will allow you to establish an open pharynx before bringing focus into the tone and singing the vowel sound.

Sing the "uh" sound and then position your tongue in the proper position for each of the following vowels as follows:

Uh – A, Uh – E,   Uh – I,   Uh – O,   Uh – U

Sing these repetitively on a single breath and focus on keeping the open throat while starting with the "uh" and transitioning to each vowel sound. Once this gets easier you while be able to open your throat using a silent "uh" position quickly and move the tongue and lips into position to sing the vowel with ease. This must become second nature for you and with this you will take your singing to the next level.

The Vibrato Technique

Vibrato is a wavering of the voice slightly higher and lower in pitch and this will create a full vocal sound. When you add vibrato to your singing it will give your voice character, personality and a touch of class. I like to think of vibrato as the icing on the cake. Let's learn how to add and control vibrato in your voice now. There is a hidden benefit of having a great vibrato. When vibrato is happening naturally in your voice it means that you are singing properly. Vibrato is a sign of good vocal technique. The added bonus is that it sounds great too!

Once you master your singing vibrato you'll be able to connect with many areas of your voice from low to high and your voice will gain a sense of balance. Vibrato happens when your voice varies quickly slightly higher and lower. It is a small wavering of the pitch that is just semi tones and it this makes your voice have a full tone. The two things you need to focus on to have a great vibrato are the speed and range in which you vary the waveform of your vocal pitches. Be very careful not to use vibrato to much or with too wide of a variation because this can start to sound unnatural or forced.

Here is a simple exercise that will allow you to see what vibrato feels like. Please understand that this is not a finished sound. It's an exaggerated version that will later be honed into something more natural. Lets go through this vibrato exercise:

1. Place your hands at the bottom of your chest and feel where your ribs come together in the middle. From there move your hands slightly below this point a few inches above your belly button.
2. Next sing a note on a pitch in the middle of your range. Any note you can sing comfortably.
3. As you're singing this note, push in and out gently with your hands. The key is to push in and out repetitively at a rate of around 2 to 3 times a second.

Listen to how your voice wavers, this is similar to the sound of singing vibrato. I know this is not exactly singing vibrato naturally but it will get you to understand and feel the vibrato sensation and it will start to come more naturally as you keep practicing this technique.

Chapter 14
Vocal Exercises Level 2

Now its time to challenge your voice and take it to the next level, this vocal exercise routine contains more advanced exercises that will help expand your range and tone. Again make sure to use the audio backing tracks so you can hear how each exercise should sound and you can follow it up to expand your range.

1 – Seven Staccatos on One Note

For your first exercise in this level you will be singing seven notes on one pitch up a major scale. You will be singing these notes in staccato, staccato by definition means "cut short or detached" which means you sing the note and stop the sound quickly and each note will sound detached or separated from the next. You need to support each note with your abs singing each note with power as well.

Sing the following vocal sounds while practicing this exercise.

Ha Hea He Ho Hoo

2 – Feel the Vibration

This exercise will help you sing your vowels and also get you to focus your vocal tone to the front of your face and not in your throat. You should feel a vibration and tingle in the front of your face and lips. Hold your lips together as you start each sound on the "M" and really get the vibration generated with the lips closed before following into the vowel sound. You will sing all five sounds on each note along with the backing track up a full octave.

Sing the following vocal sounds while practicing this exercise.

Ma – May – Me – Mo – Moo

3 – Jaw Dropping

You will be doing basically the opposite as the last exercise here. You will drop your jaw almost in a detached manor. Open and close your mouth wide and over exaggerate the movement to get the proper technique and when you drop the jaw almost feel it detach.

Sing the following vocal sounds while practicing this exercise:

Ya – Yea – Yee – Yo – You

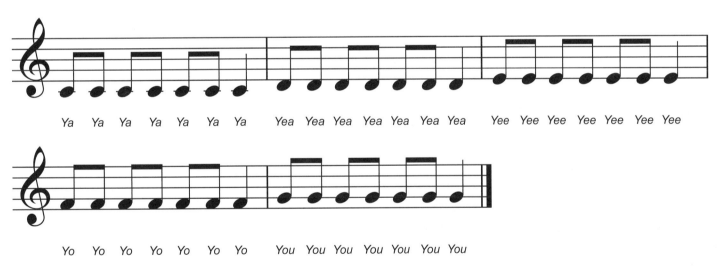

4 – Fast Tongue Flickers

Having complete control of your tongue will help you to pronounce words and vowels better making you a better all around singer. For this exercise you will sing each sound 8 times quickly. When you pronounce the L your tongue should be flickering by your front teeth. Try to keep your tongue loose and relaxed to get a fast natural movement.

Sing the following vocal sounds while practicing this exercise:

La – Lea – Lee – Lo– Lou

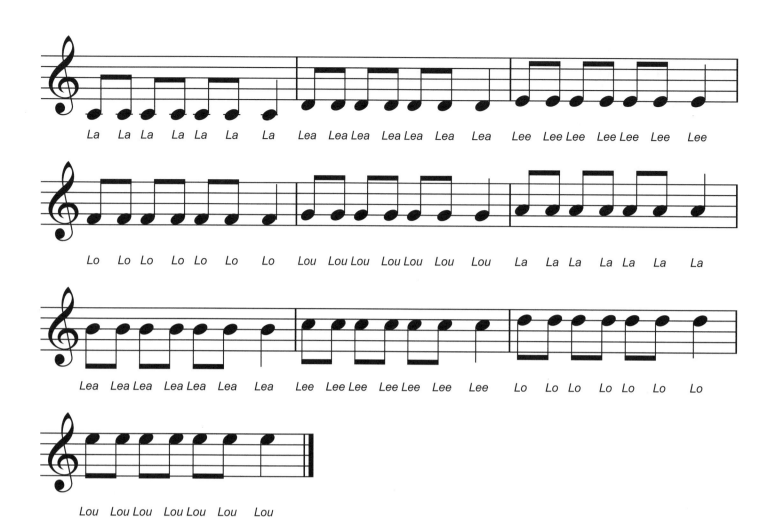

La La La La La La La Lea Lea Lea Lea Lea Lea Lea Lee Lee Lee Lee Lee Lee Lee

Lo Lo Lo Lo Lo Lo Lo Lou Lou Lou Lou Lou Lou Lou La La La La La La La

Lea Lea Lea Lea Lea Lea Lea Lee Lee Lee Lee Lee Lee Lee Lo Lo Lo Lo Lo Lo Lo

Lou Lou Lou Lou Lou Lou Lou

5 – Staccato Up Legato Down

In this exercise you will be using Staccato and Legato techniques. You learned about staccato earlier in this chapter let me explain legato to you. Legato by definition means "smooth and connected" it is basically the opposite of staccato.

Sing the following vocal sounds while practicing this exercise:

Ha – Ha – Ha – Ha – Ha aa aa aa aa

Ha Ha Ha Ha Ha - aa - aa - aa Ha Ha Ha Ha Ha - aa - aa - aa aa.....

Continue singing this exercise up an octave moving chromatically.

6 – Fast Riff Singing Exercise

As you develop into a lead singer you will need to sing fast passages in songs. This will require you to be able to control your voice and sing your vowels strong and distinctly. The following exercise will challenge your voice singing down and up the notes of a major scale using your vowel sounds.

Sing the following vocal sounds when practicing this exercise

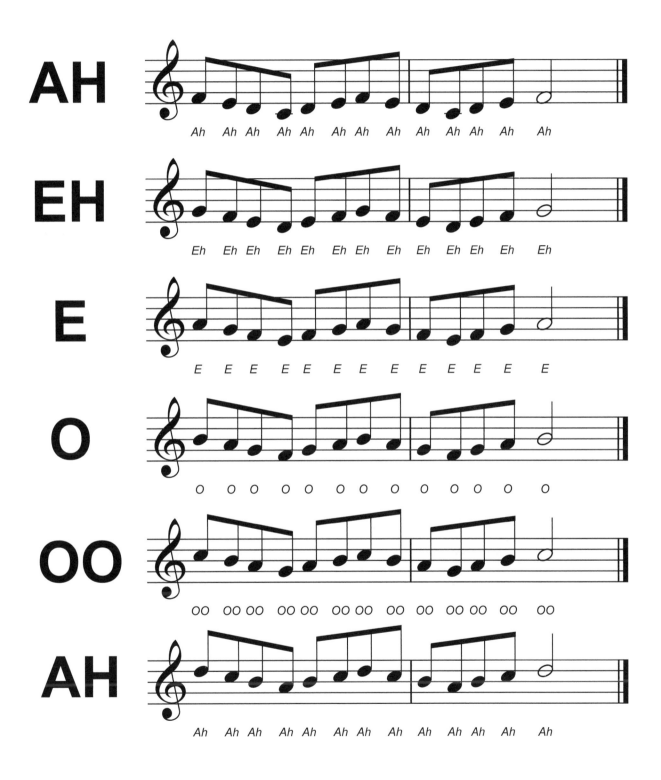

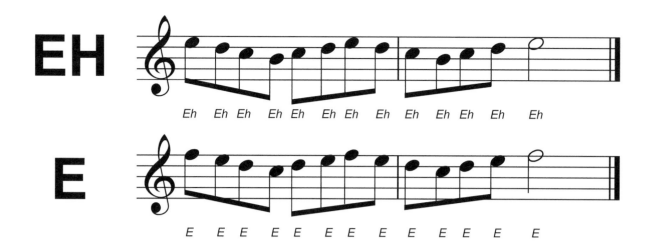

EH — Eh Eh Eh Eh Eh Eh Eh Eh Eh Eh Eh Eh Eh

E — E E E E E E E E E E E E E

7 – Single Note Legato

This exercise will help you open up on your vowels and shape your mouth correctly. You are only moving the lips slightly keeping the jaw dropped. Do not stop your vocal sound between the three vowel sounds on each note. You will be singing in legato which you learned previously is smooth and connected. So make the notes slur one into the next smoothly while shaping the vowel sounds with your mouth.

Sing the following vocal sounds while practicing this exercise:

1. **OH – AH – A**
2. **E – Oo – Ah**

1: Oh Ah A   Oh Ah A   Oh Ah A   Oh Ah A
2: E Oo Ah   E Oo Ah   E Oo Ah   E Oo Ah

A Ah Oh   A Ah Oh   A Ah Oh   A Ah Oh
Ah Oo E   Ah Oo E   Ah Oo E   Ah Oo E

8 – Soprano Arpeggio Workout

In this exercise you will sing an arpeggio in the soprano range. You will be starting on a higher pitch then past exercises, one octave higher then middle C. As you sing through the exercise and hit the higher pitches you will need to transition into your head voice, or falsetto from your full chest voice. You need to focus on the transition and make it smooth and seamless. Practice this repetitively and it will become second nature.

Sing the following vocal sounds while practicing this exercise:

Oo – Oo – E – E – E

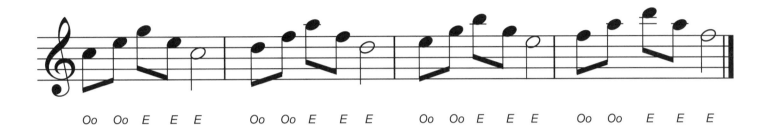

9 – Tongue Gymnastics

The sound you make when singing the letters "Gn" require you to position the back of your tongue up in your mouth. In this exercise you will sing the "Gn" sound and then follow it with a vowel sound that will make you change the position of your tongue and your mouth. This exercise is great to help you coordinate your mouth and tongue. It is quite a little tongue twister as well. I will provide two different speeds in the exercise backing track the second will be quicker and challenge you a bit more.

Sing the following vocal sounds while practicing this exercise:

Gnee – Gna - Gnee – Gna - Gnee – Gna - Gnee – Gna - Gnew

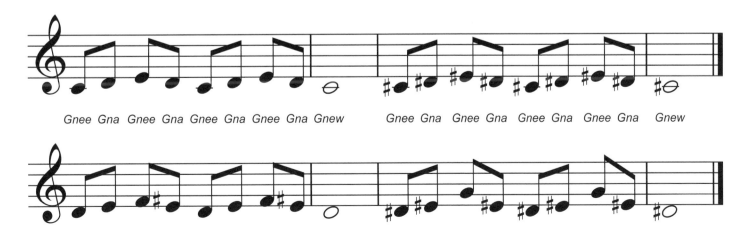

10 – Crescendo & Diminuendo

As a singer you need to sing with emotion. There are several ways to get more emotion from your voice. Two of the most common ways to filter emotion into your singing are, changing your tone and your volume. When you change your volume and sing very soft you add emotion to the lyrics. Singing softly or even in a whisper tone creates the effect like you are talking intimately to someone. On the contrast singing very loud can be emotional but in the opposite way, more angry or aggressive. You can use these techniques to add dynamics to your singing. You must become an expert at changing the timbre of your voice to advance to a higher level of singing. Changing the timbre will make the listener connect with you and feel the emotion of every word you sing. In this exercise you will sing the crescendo and diminuendo vocal techniques. Crescendo by definition means to gradually get louder and Diminuendo is to gradually get softer. You will be singing whole step intervals going soft loud soft using the notes of the C major scale. For each 3 note singing section in this exercise you start soft, crescendo louder to the 2nd note and diminuendo back to your original note. You will use the "Do – Re – Me – Fa – So – La – Te – Do" corresponding scale sound pronunciations.

11 – Triplet Pattern Singing

The following vocal exercise is a triplet pattern that goes up and down the C major scale. Triplets are three note intervals are counted as follows:

One - Trip - Let, **Two** - Trip - Let, **Three** - Tri - Let, **Four** - Trip - Let

Most counting in music is based around count in 4's and even numbers so the triplet is a variation that can give a little different feel to the music.

Sing the following vocal sounds while practicing this exercise:

1. Ahh
2. Ehh
3. E
4. O
5. Oo

1:	Ahh Ahh Ahh Ahh	Ahh Ahh Ahh	Ahh Ahh Ahh	Ahh Ahh Ahh	Ahh Ahh Ahh	Ahh Ahh Ahh	Ahh Ahh Ahh	Ahh Ahh Ahh
2:	Ehh Ehh Ehh Ehh	Ehh Ehh Ehh	Ehh Ehh Ehh	Ehh Ehh Ehh	Ehh Ehh Ehh	Ehh Ehh Ehh	Ehh Ehh Ehh	Ehh Ehh Ehh
3:	E E E E	E E E	E E E	E E E	E E E	E E E	E E E	E E E
4:	O O O O	O O O	O O O	O O O	O O O	O O O	O O O	O O O
5:	Oo Oo Oo Oo	Oo Oo Oo	Oo Oo Oo	Oo Oo Oo	Oo Oo Oo	Oo Oo Oo	Oo Oo Oo	Oo Oo Oo

12 – Scale Pattern Singing

Singing patterns up and down scales is a great way to challenge your voice and help you to gain control of your pitch. In this exercise you will sing 3rds up the C major scale.

Sing the following vocal sounds while practicing this exercise:

1. A – Er – A – Er – A – Er – Ahh
2. U – E – U – E – U – Ahh

| 1: | A | Er | A | Er | A | Er | Ah | | A | Er | A | Er | A | Er | Ah |
| 2: | E | U | E | U | E | U | Ah | | E | U | E | U | E | U | Ah |

13 – Chromatic Breath Control Exercise

For this exercise you will descend down a chromatic scale starting on a High C note. There are two descending patterns you will sing in this exercise and here is the tricky part, you will not take a breath in throughout the entire exercise. You need to take a big breath in and really control your breath letting only a small amount out gradually as you sing. This may be challenging but with practice you will be able to sing all the way through on one breath.

Use the sounds underneath the staffs for the entire exercise.

1.	Ah	Ah	Ah	Ah	Ah	Ah	Ah	Ah	Ah	Ah	Ah	Ah	Ah
2.	Eh	Eh	Eh	Eh	Eh	Eh	Eh	Eh	Eh	Eh	Eh	Eh	Eh
3.	E	E	E	E	E	E	E	E	E	E	E	E	E
4.	O	O	O	O	O	O	O	O	O	O	O	O	O
5.	Oh	Oh	Oh	Oh	Oh	Oh	Oh	Oh	Oh	Oh	Oh	Oh	Oh

1.	Ah	Ah	Ah	Ah	Ah	Ah	Ah	Ah	Ah	Ah	Ah	Ah	Ah
2.	Eh	Eh	Eh	Eh	Eh	Eh	Eh	Eh	Eh	Eh	Eh	Eh	Eh
3.	E	E	E	E	E	E	E	E	E	E	E	E	E
4.	O	O	O	O	O	O	O	O	O	O	O	O	O
5.	Oh	Oh	Oh	Oh	Oh	Oh	Oh	Oh	Oh	Oh	Oh	Oh	Oh

14 – Portamento Slide Exercise

Portamento by definition means pitch sliding from one note to another. This is a common technique used in singing. This exercise will help you understand then apply this technique into your singing. You will use the Do – Re – Me sounds to sing the exercise.

Use the following vocal sound to sing this exercise:

1. Do
2. Re
3. Me

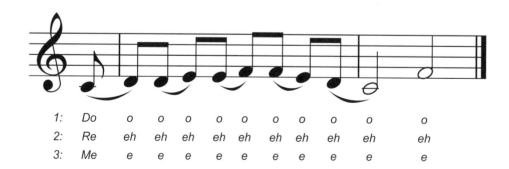

1:	Do	o	o	o	o	o	o	o	o	o
2:	Re	eh	eh	eh	eh	eh	eh	eh	eh	eh
3:	Me	e	e	e	e	e	e	e	e	e

Chapter 15
Arpeggio Vocal Exercises

In this section you will sing a series of arpeggio exercises. Let me start by explaining what an arpeggio is and the most used ways of applying them in music. An arpeggio by definition is "the notes of a chord sounded separately." Musicians and singers use arpeggios in songs several ways, on instruments such as guitar and piano musicians play arpeggios for the chords of the song to create a full sound. A guitarist also may use arpeggios in lead sections. Bass players use arpeggios to create bass lines that structure the chords in the song. You as a singer will use arpeggios in a few different ways as well. For creating melodies you will use the notes of an arpeggio as your tone centers or the most dominant tones to sing in your melodies. You also will use arpeggios to create harmonies to add dimension to songs.

The following exercises will challenge your vocal skills and help train your ear to hear and sing arpeggios. The better you hear, understand and sing arpeggios the easier it will be for you to apply them into your singing.

Exercise 1 – Major Triad

Learning to sing the major triad is probably the most important vocal exercise you will learn. The reason is it contains the three most important notes you need to be able to sing, the root, the 3rd and the 5th. These three notes also are the most used notes in singing harmonies. It is essential for you to learn how to sing a major triad so you can apply them as vocal harmonies. The better you can sing a major triad the better you will be at singing harmonies. We will get more into singing harmonies in another lesson but lets get started with your first arpeggio exercise now. You will sing up and down the major arpeggio, the pattern you will sing is the following degrees of the major scale, 1 – 3 – 5 – 3 – 1.

Sing the following vocal sounds while practicing this exercise.

1. La – La – La – La - La
2. Lee – Lee – Lee – Lee – Lee
3. Ba - Be – Bi – Bo - Boo
4. Ma - Me – Mi – Mo - Moo

```
1:  La    La La   La   La
2:  Lee   Lee Lee Lee  Lee
3:  Ba    Be  Bi   Bo   Boo
4:  Ma    Me  Mi   Mo   Moo
```

Exercise 2 – Major Triad Descend

For this exercise you will sing down a major triad. The notes you will sing will be the 5th, 3rd, and root of the major scale. I will give you the root to start each time and I want you to envision the 5th higher note, which will be your first singing note. It is important for you to start being able to sing the 5th and 3rd pitches by ear because these will be the most used notes for harmonies. The pattern you will sing in this exercise is the following degrees of the major scale, 5 – 3 – 1.

Sing the following vocal sounds while practicing this exercise.

1. Day and Night
2. Me May Mo

Exercise 3 – Major Arpeggio with Octave

When you play a major scale through all seven notes the next note higher is the root note again one octave higher. So an octave is the eighth note in the scale that is why it has the prefix "Octa" like in an octagon it has eight sides.

In this singing exercise you will sing up the major arpeggio and add the octave note as well. This will take you through a wide range spectrum as you sing through the intervals in the exercise.

Sing the following vocal sounds while practicing this exercise. Each should be used for the entire exercise.

1. La – La – La – La – La – La – La
2. Lee – Lee – Lee – Lee – Lee – Lee – Lee

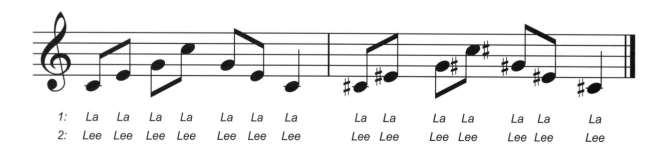

Exercise 4 – Minor Arpeggio

As you learned in the beginning of this chapter arpeggios are the notes of a chord sounded separately. So a minor arpeggio would be the notes of a minor chord. A minor chord combines the 1st, flatted 3rd and 5th notes of a major scale. The 3rd degree is a powerful note because this note makes a chord sound happy or sad which is major and minor. Major chords have a happy sound while minor chords have a sad or melancholy tone. Songwriters use these chords to create emotions in the music, if they were writing a song about a relationship breakup you can bet there would be minor chords but if the song were about finding the love of your life you would probably hear major chords. In this same fashion when you are creating a vocal melody you can use the notes of a major or minor arpeggio.

In the following exercise you will sing up and down a minor arpeggio, notice the sad overtone this arpeggio has and let that sink into your ears.

Sing the following vocal sounds while practicing this exercise. Each should be used for the entire exercise.

1. La – La – La – La – La – La – La
2. Lee – Lee – Lee – Lee – Lee – Lee – Lee

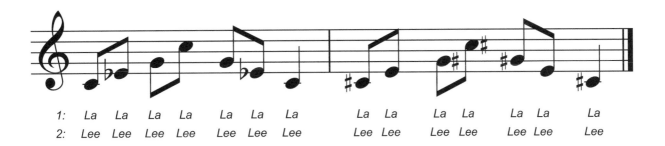

Exercise 5 – Major 7th Arpeggio

Major and minor arpeggios outline the three note basic major and minor chords. I call these the small form chords. Major 7th arpeggios outline a full four note chord which will contain the major arpeggio 1st, 3rd and 5th scale degrees but also add a 7th degree note. Adding the 7th tone into a melody will give it a more jazzy sound. Once you go through the exercise try to experiment with the arpeggio and create some melodies. Just sing the four notes and mix it up in a random order that you think sounds good. Use your ears to guide you. These are exercises to improve your singing but the core of what you are learning here is the nuts and bolts for creating melodies and song writing in general.

For the "E – Ah" your mouth goes from a smile to a drop jaw. For the "I – O" start with a smile then go to an O rounded mouth shape.

Sing the following vocal sounds while practicing this exercise.

1. E – Ah – E – Ah – E – Ah – E – Ah – E

2. I – O – I – O – I – O – I – O – I

| 1: | E | Ah | E | Ah | E | Ah | E | Ah | E | E | Ah | E | Ah | E | Ah | E | Ah | E |
| 2: | I | O | I | O | I | O | I | O | I | I | O | I | O | I | O | I | O | I |

Exercise 6 – Minor 7th Arpeggio

The major 7th arpeggio was a major arpeggio with the 7th degree added, in the same fashion the minor 7th arpeggio is the minor arpeggio with the flat 7 note added. So from a major scale the minor 7th arpeggio is the 1st, flatted 3rd, 5th and flatted 7th notes of the major scale. Because it is minor it will have the sad tone.

Be creative with this arpeggio as well, sing the notes in a random order and create your own melodies. Always try to be creative with your music.

Sing the following vocal sounds while practicing this exercise.

1. E – Ah – E – Ah – E – Ah – E – Ah – E

2. I – O – I – O – I – O – I – O – I

| 1: | E | Ah | E | Ah | E | Ah | E | Ah | E | E | Ah | E | Ah | E | Ah | E | Ah | E |
| 2: | I | O | I | O | I | O | I | O | I | I | O | I | O | I | O | I | O | I |

Exercise 7 – Dominant 7th Arpeggio

The dominant 7th arpeggio is sort of a hybrid between a major and minor. It has a major 1st – 3rd and 5th but also adds a flatted 7th tone giving this arpeggio a distinct sound. Really listen to the sound the notes create and let that sink into your ears. The more you can train your ear to hear these tones the better you will be able to sing them. Ear training is a very important thing to work on to become a great singer.

Sing the following vocal sounds while practicing this exercise.

1. E – Ah – E – Ah – E – Ah – E – Ah – E
2. I – O – I – O – I – O – I – O – I

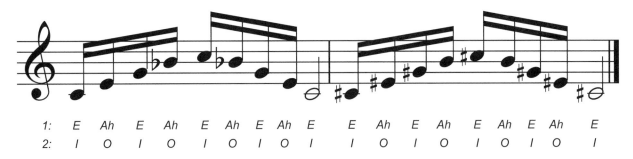

Exercise 8 – Major Arpeggio Triplet Pattern

This is a triplet pattern ascending and descending a major arpeggio. When practicing this exercise you can move higher chromatically and challenge your voice a bit more.

Sing the following vocal sounds while practicing this exercise.

La – La – La – La – La – La – La – La – La

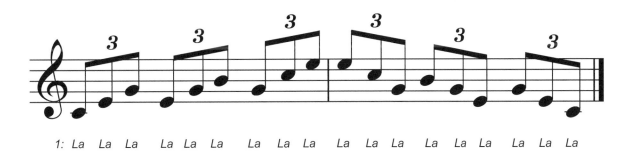

Practice this example forwards and backwards.

Exercise 9 – Minor Arpeggio Triplet Pattern

This exercise is very similar to the previous one. The only difference is you will be singing up and down a minor arpeggio in a triplet pattern. Remember that minor is a sad or melancholy sound.

Sing the following vocal sounds while practicing this exercise.

La – La – La – La – La – La – La – La – La

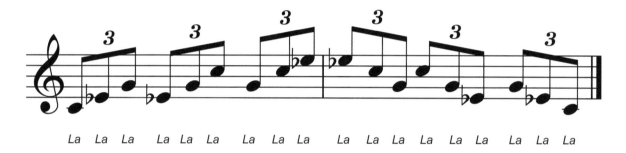

La La La   La La La   La La La   La La La La La La La La La

Practice this example forwards and backwards.

Assess Your Voice

When you first started this course I asked you to assess your voice to see what your highest and lowest notes you could sing were and asked you to record a song you felt comfortable singing. Now it's time to check and see your progress.

1. *Use an instrument to check your range and see what the lowest and highest notes you can sing are. Compare this to when you first started the course and hopefully you have seen this expand.*

2. *Record the same song you sang at the beginning of the course. As you start to have better technique you should also see an improvement in the tone and quality of your voice.*

It is important to continuously asses your progress and analyze your strengths and weaknesses to become the best singer you can be.

Chapter 16
Singing Harmonies

Singing vocal harmonies will add an extra finishing touch to a song. It makes it sound full and musically rich. You can hear vocal harmonies on the chorus to almost every song and some bands layer them on thick like Queen, Journey and the Beatles. I am going to teach you to sing harmonies in this lesson. Harmonies almost seem to be invisible on some tracks, yet on others, they seem to make the whole song. Most music you hear on the radio is filled with harmonies. A great harmony can take a track to the next level.

If you listen closely to the vocal tracks on most pop songs, you'll find tons of harmonies. You'll not only hear them on the chorus but scattered throughout the rest of the track too. Most vocalists like to stick a harmony on a couple of lines throughout the song, not just the chorus. A lot of the time, it's layered in the background, just lifting the line without making it too obvious. Doubling and singing the same line an octave above or below is also vary effective in bringing something extra to the line without having a full blown harmony there. Many artists will double their vocal lines in the recording studio. You need to be careful not to get too carried away adding harmonies because when you preform live you want to sound close to your recordings.

The two harmonies used most are 3rds and 5ths so I am going to focus on these first. You have been singing 3rds and 5th in the vocal exercises you have been singing but now you will stack the notes together and hear how they harmonize.

3rd Harmony

To sing a 3rd harmony you sing the note three notes up the scale from the note you want to harmonize. The starting note is considered the root note. For example to sing a 3rd harmony from C you would sing an E note.

C – D – E   3rd – E
1   2   3   Root – C

The key of C major has no flats or sharps so it is easy to find harmony notes for this key. All the other keys will contain some sharp or flat notes so you will need to learn some music theory to find harmonies in other keys.

Sing the following 3rd harmonies along with the backing track to get your harmonies rocking.

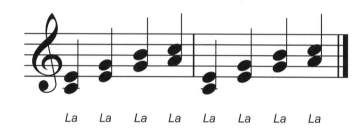

La   La   La   La   La   La   La   La

5th Harmony

To sing a 5th harmony you sing the note five notes up the scale from the note you want to harmonize. The root and 5th are the most powerful notes in the major scale and they even have their own chord the "Power Chord". The root and 5th are found in just about every chord, which makes this harmony a great one to use in singing.

C – D – E – F – G   5th – G
Root   2   3   4   **Fifth**   **Root – C**

The key of C major has no flats or sharps so it is easy to find harmony notes for this key. All the other keys will contain some sharp or flat notes so you will need to learn some music theory to find harmonies in other keys.

Sing the following 5th harmonies along with the accompanying backing track.

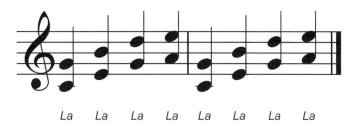

La   La   La   La   La   La   La   La

3rds and 5ths Exercise

You need to train yourself to sing 3rds and 5ths so you can harmonize. In this exercise I am going to give you the root note and demonstrate the 3rd and 5th then you will sing these harmonies against the root note. The more you do this in a repetitive manor the better your ear will be trained to sing the harmonies. My favorite saying is "repetition is the mother of skill."

Stacked Harmonies

You don't have to only use one note to create a harmony there can be multiple notes stacked together creating a lush vocal sound. When you stack notes it creates a chord, which is why it sounds so full. In this example I am going to have you sing 3rds and 5ths together with the root note so you can hear the effect. As you continue to sing these harmonies will become second nature to you and you will be able to sing 3rds and 5ths by ear at will.

					5th − G
C − D − **E** − F − **G**					**3rd** − E
1	2	**3**	4	5	**Root** − C

Sing the following stacked harmonies along with the accompanying backing track.

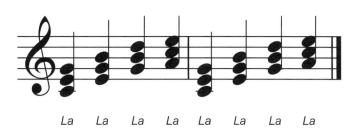

La   La   La   La   La   La   La   La

Chapter 17
Song Writing

As a lead singer you have many options of ways to let your voice be heard. You can sing in a cover band, which is playing other bands music. You can target a specific genre of music rock, blues, pop, top 40 and such. You can also choose to be a tribute band where you only play one band's music and almost mimic that band. Some common bands people tribute are The Beatles, Pink Floyd, Led Zeppelin and Ozzy.

You may also evolve into an original artist yourself and write your own music. Writing music isn't easy for many musicians, it may take several years to find your niche and create your own style. In this section I am going to go through several of the main components that will help you become a songwriter and a series of creative exercises to help get you on your way to become a songwriter. Keep in mind that as a songwriter you will be ever evolving and your own creativity must shine though so be prepared to dig deep into your emotions.

Lets start by going through what makes a song. If you don't play an instrument you will have a more difficult time writing the actual music sections although it is not impossible. Even if you don't play an instrument you must have the knowledge of how songs are constructed so you can create your own melodies and lyrics and also communicate with all the other musicians in your band more effectively.

Song Construction

When writing a song there are common sections that you should learn about that will help you structure some great songs. The two sections that make the main song structure are the verse and chorus. All the other sections give the song dynamics and diversity. The verse usually tells the story of a song while the chorus is a repetitive catchy section that seems to brainwash the listeners at times. The following are the most common sections that are used to write songs:

Introduction
The introduction or "intro" is a unique section that comes at the beginning of the song. It usually builds up suspense for the listener. The intro may be based around the chords used in the verse, chorus, or bridge, or main riff of the song.

Verse
The verse tells the story of the song. When two or more sections of the song have the same music with different lyrics these sections are most likely considered the verses. Each verse section can have the same melody and rhythm; it is the lyrics that will vary. Often a verse has a chord structure that is longer before repeating giving more time to tell the story. A song can have many verses.

Pre-Chorus
When a song incorporates a pre-chorus it occurs after the verse and functions to connect the verse to the chorus. Often when the verse and chorus use the same chord structure the pre-chorus will introduce a new section in order to make the chorus have more impact.

Chorus

The chorus or "refrain" is the repetitive catchy section of a song. The chorus often contrasts the verse melody and rhythm to create a higher level of dynamics. When two or more sections of the song have basically, identical music and lyrics, these sections are most likely considered the chorus. A chorus usually has a chord structure that is short and repeats often to give it a catchy effect. A chorus usually has a strong focus on the root chord or the chord that is the name of the key. Sometimes the chorus is repeated at the end and at the beginning of a song.

Bridge

A bridge is a section that connects two parts of a song. The bridge usually differs from the verse and the chorus in its chord structure and lyrics. Unlike a verse or chorus section, a bridge does not always contain lyrics. A bridge may be performed as an instrumental section with a melody.

Lead Section

A lead section or "solo" is a section designed to showcase an instrument. The lead section may take place over the chords from the verse, chorus, or bridge, or over a standard solo backing progression, such as a 12-bar blues progression. In some cases the melody that the singer sang for the chorus is played with embellishments such as bends, scale runs and arpeggios to form a lead section.

Break Down

A break down is a section that lowers the dynamic level to set up a higher dynamic section often the chorus. The break down is usually an instrumental section and often has a build up at the end. In metal music, breakdowns are used to energize the crowd with a heavy, rhythmic section.

Outro

An outro is a short ending section to the song. Often the outro is the chorus of the song repeated with layered vocal and instrumental melodies called the "chorus out."

Writing Lyrics

Lyrics are one of the most common lead singer contributions to a song. Most times the lead singer writes the lyrics because it is you who is singing them and your emotion is put into the delivery as well. There is no one way that you should write lyrics that is correct, there are many ways to craft interesting and catchy lyrics. I recommend that you buy a nice notebook or journal and start writing all your ideas and lyrics in one place. It's a great way to keep track of all your creations and one day when you become a big super-star people will pay millions of dollars for it ☺ Here are a few exercises that you can try to help kick start your lyric writing.

Analyze Lyrics from Some of your Favorite Artists

You can learn a lot about writing lyrics by studying your favorite artists work and taking note to the process they use. Not that you should copy them directly but this will give you many ideas to use in your own way. Find the things you like that they do and put your own twist on the technique. Lets get into the exercise and start you on your lyric writing path.

Exercise 1

Gather the lyric sheets for 10 of your favorite songs. I suggest that you print them out so you can write on them but you can import them into a word document if you prefer. Take the lyrics one song at a time and mark the different song sections using the outlined sections you just learned. Next take note of the following things within each song:

- Does it have a repeating chorus lyric?
- Are there rhyming words? If so take note to where they are, every other line, every line, or at the end of each paragraph.
- Is the writer using descriptive words, such as "The night was cold as ice" or " She was as beautiful as a Summer sunset"
- Is the writer being direct or more abstract?
- Can certain lines have multiple meanings?

A great songwriter can write lyrics that many people can relate to in different ways. Here is an example:

 "I'm going to miss you when you're gone. Everything in life happens for a reason"

This lyric can be interpreted in multiple ways:

1. It could be about a breakup
2. It may be about someone you loved passing.
3. It could be someone you cared about is moving away.

Creating imagery when writing lyrics. Paint a mental picture, It leaves more room for creativity around any power words you use. Start with a power word and find other ways to express it using imagery. For example, "joy." Instead of just saying joy, you could say something like "The sun fills my sole! I feel light on my feet. I'm flying high, as I'm walking down the street."

Tell a Stranger's Story

Most people only have so many life experiences to write about. I found a great way to write and have a limitless amount of topics is to write about is to tell someone else's story. It is also a great way to expand your imagination. Here is the exercise. Go to a public place that will have many people like a park or the mall. When you see an interesting person walk by think about what they are feeling. Even though you don't know the person use your imagination to create a story. For example I would sit on a bench at the mall, and one day I saw an older lady walking by very slow and looking sad. I starting think maybe her husband passed and she is lost in life. She is going to places that she went with him before to remember the good times. Then I wrote a whole song about this topic.

Exercise 2

Go to a public place and try this exercise. Pick a person out and try to envision what they are thinking, what is going on in their life, what problems they may have or what great things are happening for them. Bring your journal or notebook and write away. You don't need to make everything perfect at this point this is just for ideas and topics to write songs about. Once you get home in your own environment you can fine tune all the lyrics and craft some great songs! Be very creative and use a lot of descriptive words.

Swap Lyrics with the Pros

Take a few of your favorite songs and re-write lines in the song, either try to get the same meaning using different words or change the meaning of the song completely. This exercise will help you write songs to the level of your favorite artists. Here is an example:

<u>Original Lyrics</u>

What do you do
When it's falling apart
And you know it was going on
From the very start

Do you close your eyes
And dream about me

A girl in love
With a gleam in her eye
I was a younger boy
All dressed in white
We're older now

Do you still think about me

<u>New Lyrics</u>

What do you do
<u>if you can't see the light</u>
And you know it was going on
<u>But you can't stand to fight</u>

Do you close your eyes
<u>And change the game</u>

A girl in love
<u>Looking to the sky</u>
I was a younger boy
<u>Can you give it one more try</u>
We're older now

Do you still think about me

Exercise 3

For this exercise you will pick some of your favorite songs and do the exercise as I did. Take the lyric sheets for each song and cross out every other line. Next write lyrics for each crossed off line. This will really help you to get a feel for your lyric writing and spark many creative ideas. Make sure to write these into your journal as well.

Creative Writing Exercise

You need to constantly push yourself to be creative. The more you write creatively the better you will get at lyric writing. You will also begin to get your own style formed. I love doing the following exercise with students because it blows me away how creative people can get. Here is what you are going to do:

Exercise 4

1. Get a pad and a writing utensil.
2. Think of a topic to start off with, make it something broad not too specific such as "Love", Relationships", "going on a vacation" or anything else you like.
3. Start writing as fast as possible anything that comes to your mind for one-minute straight. You MUST not stop and write quickly.

The objective here is to write faster then you can consciously think. You will probably be amazed when you read back what you wrote. You can use these as lines in your lyrics. This exercise really helps you to start thinking creatively with lyrics.

Choose and Use Your Words Wisely

If you are writing lyrics you need to grow your vocabulary. Just as a painter uses many colors to paint a picture you should have many words to craft your lyrics. I used to look through the dictionary for cool words that are not used often and add them into my songs. I called them my "Power Words." Become a professional wordsmith and take it to the next level.

Exercise 5

I want you to start a list of your own "Power Words." Everyday look through the dictionary and pick a few new words. Use every new word you choose as many time as you can during that day in conversations with anyone you come in contact with.

Describe you Emotions

As a lyricist you will need to use words to describe ideas, objects and emotions. Using descriptive words can put a fresh new twist on your lyrics.

Exercise 6

For this exercise you are going to describe emotions. Pick an emotion and add descriptive word(s) before each. Here is a list of some emotions to use.

Fear – Sorrow – Happiness – Sadness - Anger – Joy – Love – Pain

Here are a few examples to start you off. "Heart Wrenching Sorrow," "Blissful Love." Make as many as you can and add them to your notebook or journal.

Chapter 18
Music Theory for Singers

No matter if you play an instrument or not you need to have some basic music theory knowledge to help you understand the music better and communicate with other musicians effectively. I'm not going to get too deep here, I'm just going to give you the basics that every musician or singer should know.

Timing

You have done a bunch of singing exercises that were focusing on pitch and phonation now you will learn about timing. Timing refers to the duration you hold a note for. Here are the most common notes.

Whole Note

The whole note has a hollow head and no stem. It receives 4 beats of sound. So if you were to sing a whole note you sing and count 1 – 2 – 3 - 4 as you hold the pitch.

Half Note

A half note receives 2 beats. It has a hollow head and a stem. Half notes get 2 beats of sound. To count half notes you would count 1 - 2 then on 3 - 4 you sing the next note.

Quarter Notes

Quarter notes have a solid head and a stem. Quarter notes receive 1 beat of sound. Counting quarter notes you sing a note on each number 1 – 2 – 3 – 4.

Eighth Notes

An eighth note has a solid head, stem and a flag. It received ½ beat of sound. It also introduces you to a new counting. Instead of counting 1 – 2 – 3 – 4 as you did for all the other notes you will count 1 + 2 + 3 + 4 +

Measures

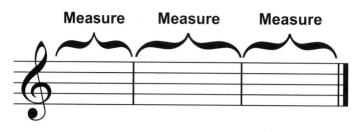

In music notation, a measure (or bar) is a section of the music and a segment of time within a song. Vertical lines called bar lines separate the music staff into small sections. All the measures within a song contain the same number of beats, which is depicted by the top number of the time signature at the beginning of the song. The most common timing in modern music is 4/4, which means there will be 4 beats in every measure. You may have hear someone counting 1 – 2 – 3 – 4 before a song starts, this is to set the tempo and timing for the song.

As a singer you need to know the time signature for every song you sing so you know if it is divided into 4 beat sections (most common) or another timing variation.

Exercise

Try counting 1 - 2 – 3 – 4 along with your favorite songs. Most of the popular songs you hear on the radio are in 4/4 timing so this will work perfectly counting in 4's. Counting along with songs will help you to understand timing in music better.

Song Progressions

A song progression or chord progression is a series of chord put together to form a song. Many songs have several chord progressions that make the song structure. To really understand the song structure you need to have knowledge of all the major scale keys. This includes knowing how many sharps or flats that are included in each specific key. In this course I am not going to go deep into this theory but I do recommend that you learn music theory so you can completely communicate with other musicians.

Musical Alphabet

The first thing you need to know is the musical alphabet, which includes the following letters:

A – B – C – D – E – F - G

After G the next letter goes back to A in a circle type fashion. So these seven letters make the complete musical alphabet.

Numbers for Chord Progressions

When musicians refer to chord progressions they usually reference them by the number of the scale degree that corresponds to the letter. For instance, if you were in the key of C major, C would be the 1 chord, D would be the 2 chord, E would be the 3 and so on. So if you wanted to know what chords were in a 1 – 4 – 5 progression in C it would be as follows."

C Major Scale - C – D – E – F – G – A – B – C
1   4   5

So C – F – and G are the chords that make a 1 – 4 – 5 progression in the key of C. In the same fashion you can figure out the chords that make all variations of chord progressions. The one thing that would be a variable is if certain keys have sharps or flats, and for this you will need to study music theory to learn this information.

Chapter 19
Metal Screaming Techniques

In this section I am going to teach you a series of metal screaming techniques. You may find a few that fit you best so don't feel like you have be master all of them. The most important thing to remember when trying any of these techniques is that you should not feel ANY strain or pain in your throat. The most popular metal scream is the "Fry Scream." I am going to start with this one and then teach you a few others that have their own unique sounds.

Fry Techniques Scream

A Fry Scream is when your vocal folds come together to form a passive wall. The sound should not come from your throat but more from your soft palate in the top of you mouth.   Remember that little kid in the movie "The Shinning" looking in the mirror and saying "Red Rum" in that gravel voice? Lets start with this, mimic that sound, you can even move your index finger up and down if it helps. You should be able to make this sound fairly easy. Now as you are saying this make the sound more like a duck quacking, this may require you to change your mouth shape more long and your face muscles should tighten a bit as well.

The three steps to achieving the Fry Scream are as follows:

1. **Sound & Placement** – First you must get the basic sound, I hope that the Red Rum exercise we just did helped you to get the basic sound started. You don't need to be loud with this sound at this point. The biggest problem people have is when they try to push to hard and give the sound power too quickly. You need to generate the sound before you can project it. So get your demon finger pumping and give me some red rum!

Now lets talk about placement. The Fry Scream should be sounded in the soft palate at the roof of your mouth. This is also where the falsetto singing voice comes from. I have students start with a comfortable falsetto singing note then convert it to the red rum sound. It may not be easy at first so don't get discouraged quickly. Remember the sound must resonate from your cheek area in the middle of your face. With practice you should be able to sound the basic fry sound.

2. **Consistency** - Once you are able to make the fry sound the next step if to keep it even for a period of time. What I want you to do is hold the fry sound and count to 20. Make sure to take a deep breath and don't let out too much air all at once.

3. **Add Power and Character** – Once you can carry on the fry sound for a period of time you need to put you personality into the scream and give it your own character. You can create unique sounds by shaping your face and mouth differently. As you get the basic fry sound try opening and closing your mouth to different shapes and you will hear drastically different sounds coming out.

To gain more power you need to tighten your abdominal muscles. This will give you a little more push with your sound.

The Middle Scream

Find a note in the middle of your singing range that you can sing comfortably with ease. Sing the note and while you are singing it compress your diaphragm (tighten your abdominal muscles) like as if you were doing a sit up. So as you start singing the note clean tighten your diaphragm and let the note turn into the scream tone. You should open your mouth wider as you do this as well and your face muscles will tighten as well. You may feel the note in your throat a little but it should mainly come from your chest.

Once you can do this scream you can do a variation of the scream by toning it down a bit. In this fashion you can get a bit more tone in each note even though you are still screaming.

Barking Low Screams

An easy way to describe how to sound the Barking Low Scream is to literally think like a dog! Your mouth shape is more in an "O" shape for this scream. I also find it better to tilt your chin and head downward; this helps get the perception focusing on the lower toned note as well.

Inhale Screams

A good way to get your body used to this type of sound is to plug your nose and mouth and breathe in and take note to how your chest and throat react. This is the same way it should move as you do the Inhale Scream. So as you breathe in create the scream sound and try to get your first Inhale Scream sounds. One downside to this scream is that it is difficult to pronounce consonants which makes it harder for people to understand what you are saying.

You can also try changing the shape of your mouth as you do this scream and the tone of the sound will change as well.

Metal Singing Tips

- Be a chameleon! If you have a favorite metal singer get some knowledge by listening how they sing, growl and scream and imitating their sounds with your voice. Make sure you are using proper technique so that you don't strain or harm your voice. Screaming, growling and singing metal music dries up your throat very fast so you must drink plenty of water, preferably warm water to keep your throat hydrated.

- You should take special care of your vocal health if you want to sing metal music because you will be doing intensive screaming and growling. It involves a certain amount of forcible singing and if you are not careful about the proper technique it can cause strain to your vocal chords or sometimes even permanent damage.

- If you feel any pain in your throat while learning to sing metal, stop immediately and rest your vocal chords. In metal singing, the sound of your voice comes mostly from the base of the throat and not by the vibration of the vocal chords. There are a number of metal singing tips, methods and exercises to follow that are covered in this book. The most important tip is to follow all instruction to the letter. You have to practice your exercises repetitively while learning how to sing metal as well as any other genre.

Chapter 20
Tips to Take Your Singing to the Next Level
Tips for Choosing Songs

Choose Songs that Force you to Sing High Notes

If one of your long-term goals is to expand your upper range, you should choose songs to sing that have one or more challenging high note sections. You need to constantly challenge yourself and push the boundaries to expand your range. Spend extra practice time on those high notes to make sure you are challenging your upper range and executing the notes properly. The perception of coming down to sing a high note can help you to hit these notes more effectively.

Choose Songs that Force Transition Singing

One thing that many singers have trouble with is "Transition Singing" (the passageway between your middle voice and your head voice), you should be working on songs that have one or more notes right in the middle of your transition area. Being able to naturally transition from your chest voice to a head voice or falsetto will make you a better all around singer. Practicing these more difficult notes will give you the confidence to sing any song in your repertoire.

Choose Songs that Include Holding a Note for an Extended Period of Time

If you have been doing your breathing exercises it's time to take it to the next level. You should continuously be working on breathing exercises in new and challenging ways. For example, choose a song to practice that will require you to hold a note in strong tone for an extended period of time. Focus on not letting too much air our quickly so you can keep a full tone note the entire length of time.

Tips to Get You Performing

Start to Perform, Even in Front of Just One Person

Sure, you perform for your voice teacher each week, but the next step on the singing ladder is to perform for other people. Start with someone you feel comfortable with, maybe a family member or close friend. The more you sing in front of people the easier it will get. Once you feel more comfortable have little concerts in your house and perform in front of more people, once you feel comfortable in front of a small group of people you will be ready to venture out in the public! One great way to get in front of larger groups of people is to search for local venues with karaoke or open mics nights. There are many places in every town that offer these nights where you can get up in front of people and show them your talents. You can also find other musicians to perform with or start a band this way.

Record Yourself Singing

Just about everyone doesn't like the sound of his or her own voice at first. Also many people are afraid of what their voice will sound like on a recording. The only way to get past that fear is to start recording yourself regularly. When you listen back to the recording you'll get to know if you're singing in tune and if you're putting real feeling into your words. Most importantly, you'll begin to make friends with your voice and all of its strong and weak points. Every voice has its strengths, and every voice is unique. By recording yourself, you can even begin to create your very own vocal style

Set your Goals High

It's also helpful to make a list of things you've always wanted to do with your voice. Knowing your specific goals or aspirations will make your job easier. For example, there may be additional exercises you can learn that are specific to a specific genre or style of singing. These can include new breathing exercises, head voice techniques, developing or straightening vibrato, building power, and loads of other "no-longer-a-beginner" tricks to try. By challenging your self with these new ideas, you may find that your voice does some amazing things that you would have never thought possible!

Shaking Out the Nerves

If you have had the experience of getting up in front of people to perform then you probably know the feeling of nervous anticipation also know as "The Jitters." As a singer it builds up as the band starts the first song and you are getting ready to belt out your first lyrics. I'm not sure there is any proven cure for stage freight but I am going to help with some tips to ease the process.

The voice is a very vulnerable instrument because it is very personal, it's like you are putting yourself out there for everyone to hear and you are right in front for everyone to see. Singing is also the most rewarding instrument because of these same reasons.

The first step you can take is to become comfortable with singing in front of small groups of your family and friends. I tell my students to start with your family because you can be most relaxed in front of them. After you have a few songs ready to sing ask your family to spend 10 minutes with you to begin your performance career. You can also ask them for some feedback on how you can improve as well. Next set up small performances for your friends. Use those same songs you sang for family for your performance and invite your closest friends over. Tell your friends you are preparing for larger performances and you need their support and feedback. Most times your friends will be really excited to help and may even ask for a promise of "Back Stage VIP Passes" when you become famous!

You can also perform for your voice instructor (if you have one) in your singing lesson. They are professionals and have most likely been there before. They would understand being shy at first, a qualified voice instructor is someone you can trust; they will have the experience and the right teaching personality to not be judgemental, and to make you feel at ease.

Practice Daily

I recommend that you practice your warm-ups and exercises from this course book at least 30 minutes a day to get real results. You can practice singing more than 30 minutes but be sure to take breaks between each 30-minute practice session so you can rest your voice. Also be aware not to push your voice too much and strain it. It is important to stop practice if you are feeling any strain or soreness in your throat, and to not practice singing when you are under the weather.

Once you practice the warm-ups and exercises you should practice you songs and performance pieces. Make it fun and exciting and challenging as well.

Song and Lyrics First, Then Work on Technique

This tip is really important when you are preparing for a performance or a vocal audition. Before you get deep into the technique of each song you need to completely know the song, I mean inside and out. This takes repetitively listening to the song.

Start by writing out the song structure on a piece of paper. This will give you the blueprint for the song. Just write it out like the following example:

Intro, verse, chorus, verse, chorus, lead section, breakdown, chorus 4 times, ending

Next you must memorize the lyrics. This takes repeatedly reading and reciting them to yourself. Listen to the recording of the song you are preparing, or even better, record an accompanist playing it so you can sing along during your daily practice time. The more you know the song the more comfortable and successful you will be singing the song. I know that after I am finished with an audition or performance my friends and family know the songs by heart too!

You should also use this as an opportunity to understand where the song came from and understand the lyrics to help incorporate emotion and feeling into your song when you sing. I find it helpful to connect the meaning of a song to something that happened in your life, this will help carry the emotion to your voice and people will be able to relate to your singing more as well.

Setting up a Solid Practice Routine

If you're not sure how to balance your singing practice routine at home, you're not alone! Many vocal students get overwhelmed trying to figure out how long to spend warming up, working on vocal technique, and running through songs. While your vocal instructor should be your first resource for determining your specific practice routine, I've outlined some tips below to get you started.

Let's look at a one-hour voice practice routine, typically for that I would recommend for one of my students who is serious about pursuing music. I've broken this into three 20-minute sections.

20 Minutes: Warm-Ups

It's very important that you start your practice session off right away with stretching and warming up the voice. Just as an athlete warms up his or her muscles and joints before a game or practice, singers need to stretch and warm up their vocal cords before a performance or practice. There are many different warm-ups included in this book for you to practice with.

20 Minutes: Vocal Techniques and Exercises

Singers must work on their vocal technique by practicing different exercises and techniques. There are many ways to help you improve your singing covered in this book. This includes vocal exercises, pitch training, interval training, harmony, arpeggio exercises and proper posture and breathing.

20 Minutes: Song study

Use this time to work on songs and have some fun! Think of songs that you are trying to make performance-ready as well. This time should be spent on:

- Learning the melody and rhythm
- Memorizing lyrics and working on good diction and pronunciation
- Mastering the vocal style and genre of the song, and making sure you are using the appropriate vocal tone
- Making the song your own by incorporating your own musical interpretation and acting technique

- Writing your own music and lyrics, time to get creative!

Record Yourself

I also recommend that you record your singing as much as possible. I know most people don't like the sound of their own voice but the more you get comfortable with your own voice and become your biggest critic the faster you will achieve your goals.

Don't Strain

Don't hurt yourself belting. Make sure you know how before you push too much. If you're tensing when you're singing and it hurts stop, re-evaluate and ask for help. You can't replace your vocal folds like you can guitar strings. If anything hurts when you're singing you should immediately stop doing it.

Have Fun!

I suppose this should really be the most important tip or trick to learning to be a lead singer. Love what you're doing, and appreciate the fact that you are taking what you love and putting the energy into improving yourself with a skill that brings happiness to others around you and you too!

Closing Words

Congratulations on completing "Rock House Lead Singer, from Start to Stage"! You should have a solid foundation built now to kick-start your singing career. As a singer you need to make practicing a daily routine. Consistent practice will ensure that you improve and take your singing to the next level. You must be focused and dedicated to make a mark with your singing. There are many singers all over the world, you need to do everything you can to be unique make yourself stick out from the rest. I hope this course really helps you achieve your goals. You should continuously push the boundaries and challenge yourself to be the best you can. I hope one day I get to see YOU onstage in concert!

Chapter 21
Vocal Hygiene for a Strong Healthy Voice

If you really want to perform at your peak you need to care for your voice properly. No amount of warming up or practice will help if you're damaging your voice with poor vocal hygiene. Use the following practices to make sure your voice is ready to rock!

Hydration, Drink Lots of Water

It cannot be overemphasized how important it is to maintain good water intake. I recommend 6 to 8 eight-ounce glasses of water a day to maintain proper hydration. Bring a water bottle with you to work or school and refill it at the water fountain. The goal is to drink until your urine is almost clear. Good water intake helps keep the lubricating mucus on your vocal cords thin, creating the ideal environment for your vocal cords to work. Coffee, tea, and most soft drinks contain caffeine that tends to lead to dehydration. I understand its not easy and you may cheat at times but it is best to avoid these altogether if possible.

Don't Smoke

It should go without saying that your entire respiratory system, from your mouth to your lungs and your heart, are affected by smoking. Inhaling hot tobacco smoke or even cool vaporized smoke can cause inflammation and swelling. There's a lot of damage that's irreversible. The best approach to smoking is to never start and to quit immediately if you're already a smoking vocalist. It is plain in simple "Smoking is really bad for singers….period!"

Control Throat Clearing

This is a common problem with many professional singers and many people that speak professionally like politicians and teachers. It is also an issue for people with excessive mucus or reflux disorders. Your doctor will give you medications to help treat these conditions if you need, but one way or another it is important that this habit is controlled.

Everyone has to clear his or her throat from time to time, but there's a proper way to do it. Some of us even clear our throats every few minutes habitually. This places a lot of wear and tear on your vocal cords and folds, slamming them back and forth roughly like the vocal fry does. Throat clearing is extremely traumatic to the vocal cords, leading to excessive wear and tear. When you feel the need to clear your throat you should try the following strategies:

1. Swallow, have a sip of water, or clear your throat silently without allowing your vocal cords to touch.

2. If you must clear your throat, do so from the top and front of the throat using the "he-" sound like in the word hello. Don't go deep with a lot of scratchiness. Drinking plenty of fluids daily keeps your throats mucus thin and less likely to require clearing.

Limit Vocal Loudness

It has been said, "everything in moderation." This is especially true when it comes to the use of your voice. Don't speak excessively; choose your words carefully. If your job involves talking on the phone all day, then rest your voice for ten minutes every 2-3 hours. This will go a long way towards easing the strain on your voice.

Don't be tempted to scream across rooms or be forced to speak beyond a comfort level in noisy environments. This will lead to hoarseness, which can compound itself, if not given enough time to heal. You should have periods of the day where you don't speak at all, treating them as rest periods. Talk at a low to moderate volume; this will sometimes mean using different strategies when there is excessive background noise (cars, parties, airplanes, restaurants). My best advice is to minimize talking in these environments. If you must talk in these situations, you should get as close to the person you are talking to as possible, preferably facing them.

Avoid shouting and screaming. There are much better ways to get people's attention, and these methods will not traumatize the vocal cords as screaming will. Examples would include using a whistle or clapping your hands.

These are the basics but there are also other techniques you can use such as placing a humidifier in your room when you sleep to combat dryness from throughout the day.

Drugs that Affect the Voice

Antihistamines/Decongestants: These drugs are commonly found in cold preparations and allergy medications. They will result in a drying effect on the vocal cords, which is detrimental. Common medications in this category include Benadryl, Tavist, Dimetapp, Sinutab, Dristan, Entex, Sudafed, etc.

Local Anesthetics medications such as Chloraseptic should be avoided. Numbing the throat with one of these sprays is an especially bad idea if you are about to perform or sing. Performing under the influence of one of these can result in vocal damage because you don't realize that you are pushing your voice too far.

Work Environment

Avoid smoke filled and dusty environments. Traveling to dry environments such as Las Vegas or Phoenix may also cause voice problems. It is best to keep a humidifier on at night, and to maintain good water intake. Airplanes are also notoriously dry environments. If you are traveling by plane a significant amount, you should increase your water intake accordingly.

If you want to become a great singer, then it is of the utmost importance that you take good care of your voice. The following are some advice to help you maintain good vocal hygiene.

More Products From Rock House!

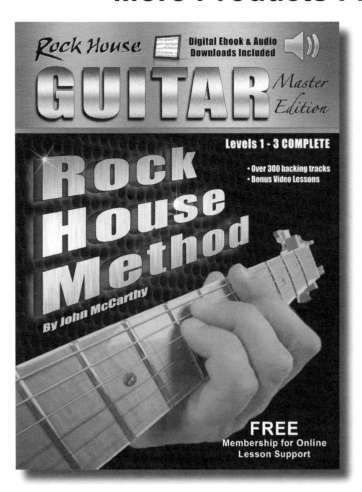

Guitar Master Edition combines all three levels of this award wining series in a complete course! Learn all the essential techniques needed to play all genres of music. Start with how to hold the guitar for comfortable playing and fast, effective learning. Next, learn picking and strumming techniques, chords, rhythm, timing, and how they are used to play popular songs. Learn melodies, scales and the basics of the blues. You will also learn lead techniques such as hammer ons, pull-offs and bends, and how to put them together to play leads and riffs! As an added bonus, included are audio backing tracks and playing examples you can download that follow each lesson and let you apply them over full band backing tracks.

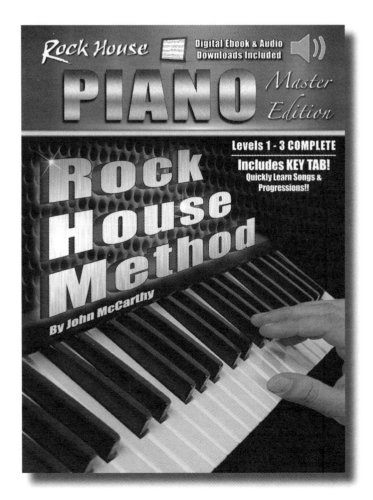

Piano Master Edition for piano or electronic keyboard, this Master Edition combines all three levels of this award wining series in a complete course! As a bonus we have included a complete "Key Tab" section that will quickly and easily show you how to play chords, progressions and entire songs. Learn all the essential techniques needed to play all genres of music. Start with proper posture and hand position. Next you will follow a gradual and progressive learning path to read music and play songs and master the keyboard. You will learn everything from classical pieces to blues progressions and challenging techniques. Learn melodies, scales and the basics of improvising. As an added bonus, included are audio backing tracks and playing examples you can download that follow each lesson and let you apply them over full band backing tracks.

"No matter if you are learning with an instructor or on your own this complete and easy to follow course with have you playing piano quickly and easily... I guarantee it!"

Bass Master Edition combines all levels of this award wining series in a complete course! Learn the essential techniques needed to play all genres of music. Start with how to hold the Bass for comfortable playing and fast, effective learning. Next learn rhythm, timing, basic bass lines and how to play along with a drummer. Learn 3rds, 5ths and octaves and how to apply them in a song, Plucking techniques including slap & pop and using a pick are covered in depth. Next learn scales from minor pentatonic to full major scales as you play them in patterns across the neck and apply them to form bass lines and write songs. All genres of music are covered from blues to rock and from jazz to metal. Learn walking bass lines, drop D tuning and syncopated bass lines and apply them over full band backing tracks to get the sensation of playing in your own band.

From theory to complete songs everything you need to MASTER BASS GUITAR in here for you!

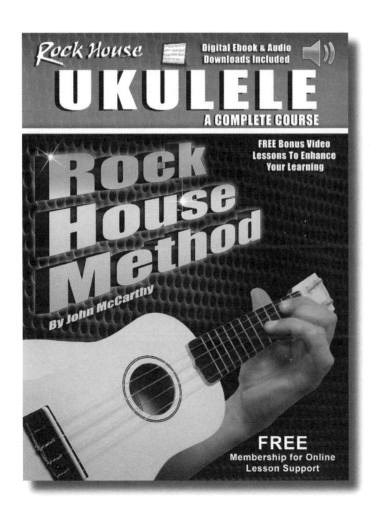

Ukulele A Complete Course has all the essential techniques needed to play all genres of music. Start with how to hold the ukulele for comfortable playing and fast, effective learning. Next, learn picking and strumming techniques, chords, rhythm, timing, and how they are used to play popular songs. Learn melodies, scales and the basics of the blues. You will also learn lead techniques such as hammer-ons, pull-offs and bends, and how to put them together to play lead riffs! As an added bonus, included is an extensive chord and scale section to further your knowledge of the ukulele. From Theory To Complete Songs Everything You Need To Play Ukulele Is Here!

About the Author

John McCarthy
Creator of
The Rock House Method

John is the creator of The Rock House Method®, the world's leading musical instruction system. Over his 30 plus year career, he has written, produced and/or appeared in more than 120 instructional products. Millions of people around the world have learned to play music using John's easy-to-follow, accelerated programs.

John is a virtuoso musician who has worked with some of the industry's most legendary musicians. He has the ability to break down, teach and communicate music in a manner that motivates and inspires others to achieve their dreams of playing an instrument.

As a musician and songwriter, John blends together a unique style of rock, metal, funk and blues in a collage of melodic compositions. Throughout his career, John has recorded and performed with renowned musicians including Doug Wimbish (Joe Satriani, Living Colour, The Rolling Stones, Madonna, Annie Lennox), Grammy Winner Leo Nocentelli, Rock & Roll Hall of Fame inductees Bernie Worrell and Jerome "Big Foot" Brailey, Freekbass, Gary Hoey, Bobby Kimball, David Ellefson (founding member of seven time Grammy nominee Megadeth), Will Calhoun (B.B. King, Mick Jagger and Paul Simon), Gus G of Ozzy and many more.

To get more information about John McCarthy, his music and instructional products visit RockHouseSchool.com.